THE POWER OF MORE

FIFTY TALES OF GRIT,
GRACE AND GOING THE EXTRA MILE

R MANOJ KUMAR

notionpress.com

INDIA • SINGAPORE • MALAYSIA

ISBN

Hardcase 979-8-90510-915-7
Paperback 979-8-90451-289-7

Contents

Greed or Growth: The Power of More

Greed or Growth: The Power of More

The term "MORE" is controversial in today's world. To one group of people, it reflects unrestrained greed, boundless consumption, and the inescapable pursuit of material success at all costs. To another group, it reflects human potential, ongoing development, and the admirable pursuit of transcending our limitations. This book contends that the choice between these two meanings does not rest with the word itself, but with the intention, methodology, and final purpose driving us towards "more."

When a young salesperson converts a ₹600 transaction into a ₹3,000 experience by truly assisting a customer to find out what he really needed for his daughter's ceremony, is that greed or growth? When an employee with hearing impairment develops creative systems that increase his outlet's sales 4x a day while providing outstanding customer-service, is that exploitation or empowerment? When a small-town waitress recalls every customer's likes and makes mundane meals into memorable experiences, is that manipulation or mastery?

The narratives you'll find in this book propose that "MORE" is transformational when it's grounded in service, innovation, and earnest concern for others. The Power of More isn't about getting more from the world, it's about contributing more to it.

How to Use This Book

This book of 50 stories covers decades of business experience in a wide range of industries, from five-star hotels to roadside eateries, from multinational corporations to family shops, from city outlets to country towns. Each is meant to stand alone so you can open the book to any chapter and find a complete lesson. But when read consecutively, the patterns and principles will be revealed to build on one another, giving you a complete philosophy of excellence.

The protagonists in these stories—Ramesh, a Shell team member with hearing impairment, Venkateshwari the tsunami victim, the faceless Mumbai shopkeeper who returned to business after shutting up shop—are real individuals, not inspirational heroes fabricated for the purpose. They found that their conditions, constraints, and adversity could become the very bedrock on which remarkable accomplishment was built.

What you'll see as you read is that some of the most significant changes occur in the most mundane places. A forecourt at a petrol station is a testing ground for creativity. A restaurant by the highway is a classroom for service. A casual discussion of biscuits is a work of art in customer watching. This is no accident—this is how "MORE" actually operates.

A little "MORE" isn't released in boardrooms or corner offices (although it can be). It's found in everyday interactions among human beings, in everyday choices to go above and beyond, in the act of deciding to view problems as opportunities and constraints as creative challenges. It's unleashed when ordinary individuals make a choice to apply extraordinary passion to what they do, no matter what their title, education level, or circumstances.

Some will make you smile at human creativity and kindness. Others will challenge your perceptions of what is possible when individuals are well-motivated and enabled. Some will anger you as you see opportunities lost in your own organisation or life. All are designed to change your mind about what success, excellence, and purposeful work look like.

The Journey Ahead

The path through these 50 stories is ultimately a path through the development of a mindset. It starts with general observations regarding exceptional service and builds slowly an overall understanding of how individuals and organisations can overcome their perceived limitations to accomplish amazing things.

You'll meet the Shell Associate who made the art of customer observation, showing that service really starts by listening to what people require before they even ask. You'll meet the new salesperson who doubled his transaction value by asking insightful questions that allowed customers to find their full requirements. You'll see how struggling businesses are transformed by nothing more than real interaction with customers.

Over the years, these stories have crossed cultures and languages and economic contexts—from the chai vendors of Surat to that German couple in Chennai, from the auto drivers of Trivandrum to the shopkeepers of Mumbai. But they all seem to be illustrating some general principles—the power of empathy, the return on genuine care, the fact that excellence at scale can create change, and the joy to be had in refusing to have one's standards capped by "good enough".

It is not strictly a business strategy or management theory book although there are many elements of that. This is not a by-the-book of sales techniques, or customer service standards, though there will be plenty of those on offer within these pages.

It is, instead, a testament to what it means to be human, the power of making an additional collective and social effort beyond necessity—aspiring for more and creating something more than was originally intended. Some will be able to directly apply those lessons in their work, teams, or careers. Others may be inspired by this story to confront their own challenges in another way.

Some will recognize themselves—or someone they know—within these pages and be encouraged through their own battle to overachieve the expected. In that sense, the last word is simple: what we should desire for ourselves more than anything else is not to want "MORE" anything, but to give "MORE" of us.

Giving a little more focus to what we see, a little more love to our service, a bit of genius to our problems and a touch more in it for the classes to get results not only for those who get them but for all involved.

The road ahead will show you that "MORE" is not greed—it's expansion. Not just profit, but the expansion of skills, of people, of happiness, and of good. It's learning that in every usual moment there is potential for something unusual, just waiting for someone who is interested enough to see it and big-hearted enough to pass it on.

Welcome to the "MAGIC" Journey

CHAPTER 01

The Nutrichoice Story

"To know the road ahead, ask those coming back."

Chinese Proverb

When I met Benny Ezekiel for the first time to discuss a training program, he narrated an anecdote from his experience at Shell, and I begin this book with it.

I was heading to a friend's wedding when I realised I hadn't eaten since lunch, and the sun was beating down mercilessly. I felt a sharp pang of hunger, reminding me the wedding supper was still several hours off. When the fuel gauge registered below zero, I observed a Shell gas station in the vicinity, allowing me to refuel my vehicle and attend to personal needs promptly.

After topping up my tank and driving into the station, I visited the convenience store. My plan was simple: get a bottle of water to last till the wedding feast and a pack of Nutrichoice cookies, my preferred snack.

Entering, the air-conditioned coolness was a wonderful relief. The store was neatly arranged, with aisles of snacks, drinks, and travel gear. I soon found the refrigerator and stretched for a water bottle. Next, I looked for biscuits.

I looked along the shelves holding the products. There were some brand-specific cookies, chocolate bars with shiny covers intended to lure, and chips in vivid colours on attractive packaging. Though I kept looking for my preferred Nutrichoice, I noticed Marie biscuits. I looked everywhere and returned to be sure I had not missed them. I began to lose hope. Perhaps they were sold out.

Glumly realizing I wouldn't get my snack; I walked to the cash counter with just the water bottle. The young man working at the counter, maybe in his early twenties, looked over my purchase. Then something out of the ordinary happened.

Perched at the counter, he asked, "Sir, were you looking for biscuits?" "What?", I asked, surprised.

"No, were you looking for Nutrichoice?" he said, his face honest.

I found myself stunned. "Exactly. As a matter of fact, "How did you figure that out?"

He gave me a smile. "I'm sorry, sir. Many customers with similar preferences tend to choose Nutrichoice." "You noticed the Marie but didn't pick it up, so I figured you were looking for Nutrichoice."

I laughed "You guessed correctly! That's exactly what I was looking for."

The smile widened on the cashier. "Sir, the pack was redesigned recently. That's probably why you couldn't locate it," he said, guiding me to the rack.

I was stunned as he walked away. Not only did this young man identify my searching pattern, but he also provided a reasonable estimate of what I would probably enjoy based on his observations. He had risen above the bare requirements of his profession, scanning purchases to anticipate a customer's need.

I couldn't resist asking more when he came back with my Nutrichoice biscuits.

"That was first-rate customer service." I asked, " Have you been here long?"

"About eight months, sir," he remarked, glancing over the biscuit packet.

"Was there somebody who taught you to notice customers like that, or do you naturally do that?"

He grinned, clearly pleased with the question, and said, "Our management advises us to track client patterns. We get trained regularly where we go over how to be detail-oriented and anticipate needs." He passed my receipt to me. " It's one of the things that distinguishes our station from others."

Curious, I asked further. "Is everyone working on this station getting this training?"

I paid for my things, but I wasn't ready to stop this talk. "Is it effective? Do you find it makes a difference?"

He nodded fiercely. "Customers come back and ask for us by name." His eyes shone as he spoke.

His tone exuded actual pride; not pride in rivalry but pride in serving others well. He was creating relationships, if ephemeral, that somewhat brightened others' day, not just selling snacks and gasoline.

With the biscuits and water in hand, I couldn't help but smile, as I was walking back to my car. In this straightforward conversation, I observed something amazing: the way one goes the additional mile; paying attention, looking forward, exerting effort, makes an imprint that lasts. creating an experience rather than completing a task.

Getting in my car, I considered the organisations I had worked for throughout my career. The most successful ones all had in common:

they established systems to support and enable people to see the human element in every interaction.

I said to myself, merging back onto the highway, "May his tribe grow,"

I had no clue that this brief interaction at the Shell station would turn into one of my favourite images when talking about the capacity to surpass expectations; of searching for the more that is possible in all settings.

A little more effort creates a lot more impact.

CHAPTER 02

The Newbie Who 5X'd His Sales

"He who asks is a fool for five minutes.
He who does not ask remains a fool forever."

Chinese Proverb

I've led hundreds of sales training sessions all over India, few have had the kind of lasting impact this one did, during a workshop for a legacy lingerie brand in Chennai. The learning didn't come from my well-prepared content or role-playing sessions, but from a surprise participant who showed me the real potential of customer engagement.

The training room was crowded with veteran sales associates when a gangly teenager, barely out of boyhood, slipped unobtrusively into the back of the room. My attention was drawn to him the moment he sat down; he appeared both intimidated and keen, notebook out and pen poised.

I spoke with him during a break. "I don't think I've seen you around before."

"No, sir," he said, his tone gentle but enthusiastic. "I only began yesterday. My boss instructed me to come here and learn 'something'." He grinned bashfully.

"Your first day at work and you're in a training session?" I was impressed by his boss's initiative and his own enthusiasm to be there.

"Yes, sir. I want to learn as much as possible."

We picked up the session, covering advanced upselling and cross-selling strategies; sophisticated sales techniques that usually take months, if not years, to perfect. Throughout the afternoon, I could not help but peek at the young associate, half-expecting to see glazed eyes or confusion.

The associate's eagerness to learn shone through. There was a bright spark that promised greatness.

A week later, we met for a second session on implementation stories. The young salesperson was there fifteen minutes before time, a small detail that says a lot about character and dedication. As other people trickled in, he was seated, having some sort of quiet assurance that I had not seen previously.

After the usual introductions, I asked if anyone would like to share their experience. Most of the experienced associates avoided eye contact - a typical response when forced into the limelight. To my surprise, the newest associate's hand popped up.

"Something happened yesterday," he said, speaking more assertively than before.

The room was quiet as he started telling his story.

"A gentleman came into our store around midday. He appeared to be in a rush and somewhat tense. He told me he needed a yellow shirt and had exactly ₹600 to spend, not a rupee more. He even took out his wallet to demonstrate that he wasn't carrying extra money."

The young associate explained how he listened attentively to the customer's requirements and was able to find a few yellow shirts within minutes. Instead of presenting all possibilities, he selected the one that best matched the requirement at a cost of just ₹300, half the customer's budget.

"When I presented it to him, his face brightened. It was precisely what he had been looking for, and he visibly relaxed at the cost. That's when I recalled what you instructed us to do about making moments of connection."

Rather than heading straight to checkout, the associate inquired about the purpose of the yellow shirt. The man told him it was for his daughter's Seemantham, a South Indian ceremony marking pregnancy.

"I congratulated him on becoming a grandfather soon," the young associate went on. "He got all teary-eyed, telling me how significant this ceremony was, given that it was for his first grandchild."

The entire room was now invested, senior sales associates leaning forward to hear every word.

"I recalled our training session on thoughtful questions, so I asked politely if he had yet bought clothes for other immediate family members who were going to be at the ceremony."

The customer's expression changed instantly, a look of realisation crossed his face. He had totally forgotten that he needed something for his son-in-law as well.

"I offered to help him find something suitable, telling him we had something for all budgets," the young associate said. "We spent the next half-hour looking through various combinations."

What began as a ₹600 purchase turned into a ₹3,000 sale. The customer walked out with two shirts, two pairs of trousers, a wallet, a handkerchief, and vests, a total wardrobe makeover instead of a single product.

"The most amazing thing," the young associate stated, his eyes shining with excitement, "was how appreciative the customer was. He thanked me repeatedly for preventing him from being in a humiliating situation.

He even wanted to know my name so that he could ask for me next time."

The training room was quiet for an instant before erupting into enthusiastic applause. Even the veteran sales associates were nodding in gratitude. When the applause died down, I inquired of him, what he had gained from the experience.

"Before your training, I would have simply sold him the yellow shirt and called it success " he thought back. "I was fearful that presenting more options would irritate customers or make me appear pushy."

He stopped for a moment, collecting his thoughts.

"Now I realize that when you ask the right questions and give valuable solutions, people don't feel pushed around, they feel assisted. The customer didn't spend extra money because I persuaded him to; he spent it because I assisted him in finding out what he really needed."

At that instant, this young fellow who had been working for only a week stated one of the deepest principles of successful selling: it's not about selling products, it's about uncovering real needs through careful conversation.

What makes this tale so extraordinary is not the increase in sale value, from ₹600 to ₹3,000. It's that the young associate instinctively understood that the art of upselling is not manipulation—it's guidance. He didn't see the customer as a wallet to be emptied, but as a human being with needs to be uncovered.

His success was not a result of sales strategies but a sincere interest and need to be of assistance. He inquired to guide the customer to a decision based on discovery rather than lead them to a predetermined outcome. Through this process, he created value for all parties: the customer saved face from an embarrassing mistake, the store generated a sale, and the associate felt the satisfaction of making a positive impact.

This young man's story demonstrates that mastering the art of selling doesn't necessarily require years of experience. Sometimes, it simply requires the willingness to listen with genuine interest and the courage to ask questions that help customers discover what they truly need.

In his first week, he had already discovered something that many take years to understand: When we reveal more possibilities to customers, we don't simply sell more, we serve better.

The difference is rarely big—it's just consistent effort.

CHAPTER 03

The Service Maestro: Ulundurpet Associate Story

"A single conversation across the table with a wise person is worth a month's study of books."

Chinese Proverb

On a road trip from Chennai to Trivandrum, my daughter and I stopped for breakfast at Vasantha Bhavan, a popular restaurant at Ulundurpet. With several restaurant brands competing for attention along the highway, what set this place apart was not its menu or ambience, but a single waiter who understood the art of service like a maestro.

Our experience began the moment we approached the restaurant. The waiter greeted us near the handwash area, offered tissues with a gentle smile and seamlessly guided us to our seats with warmth and efficiency. There was no fumbling or awkwardness—just a natural flow that made us feel immediately welcome.

As we settled at our table, I expected the usual "What would you like to order?" Instead, he asked an unusual question that took us completely off guard: "May I know what mood you're in today? What do you feel like eating?"

I looked up, surprised. This wasn't the transactional interaction I was used to at highway restaurants. His question invited us to think beyond the menu items to what would truly satisfy us at that moment. It turned a simple order into a thoughtful experience.

"We're quite hungry after driving since early morning," I replied, appreciating his approach. "What would you recommend?"

He suggested the Mini tiffin, priced at ₹ 150, noticeably higher than other items on the menu, which were below ₹120. But rather than simply pushing the most expensive item, he explained that it would allow us to taste a variety of dishes without committing to full portions. His recommendation felt genuinely helpful, not like a sales tactic.

As our food arrived, I noticed how attentive he remained, observing our reactions to each dish without hovering. When my daughter took a second helping of the Rava Kesari, her delight evident in her expression, he made a mental note.

Later, as he was delivering my daughter's ghee roast, he approached with a small surprise, a complimentary katori of Rava Kesari for my daughter. "I noticed you enjoyed this, Miss," he said with a gentle smile. Her face lit up, and in that moment, a connection was formed that transcended the typical restaurant experience.

What impressed me even more was his interaction with diners at a neighbouring table. I had left a spice powder served with my idli untouched. Our observant waiter approached, noticing the hesitation.

"Sir, may I suggest you try a small amount of this podi mixed with the ghee?" he demonstrated the technique. "It enhances the flavour beautifully."

I tried it cautiously, then broke into a delighted smile. Before long, he made me order another idli and upgraded my coffee, adding an extra ₹40 to my bill effortlessly. What struck me was that this didn't feel like upselling; it felt like guidance, like sharing a joy the customer might otherwise have missed.

Before leaving, curiosity compelled me to ask this exceptional server where he had learnt such remarkable service skills.

“My asan (guru) taught me,” he replied, pride evident in his voice. The traditional Tamil word for mentor carried deep respect in his tone. “He always said that serving food is not just about filling stomachs but about creating moments people remember.”

As we continued our journey, our conversation kept returning to this encounter. What made it remarkable wasn’t elaborate decor or exotic cuisine, but rather how this single individual transformed a routine breakfast stop into a memorable experience.

He had mastered what many businesses spend millions trying to achieve: creating moments that forge emotional connections with customers. Through thoughtful observation, personalized attention, and genuine care, he had turned a simple meal into something we spoke about for days.

His approach revealed a profound understanding that customers don’t mind spending more when they feel valued and understood. The Mini Tiffin recommendation and the neighbouring table’s order upgrade weren’t pushy sales tactics; they were thoughtful suggestions born from careful observation of customer preferences.

The complimentary Rava Kesari cost little but created immense goodwill. This waiter intuitively understood the economics of customer delight: that small gestures can yield returns far greater than their cost in the form of loyalty, word-of-mouth, and return visits.

In an age of sophisticated marketing strategies and customer experience design, this humble waiter at a highway restaurant demonstrated that genuine service combined with thoughtful recommendations remains the most powerful formula for creating memorable experiences and driving higher revenue.

Clarity of purpose drives quality of action.

CHAPTER 04

The Service Recovery Expert: Ulundurpet Associate Story

"Better to light a candle than curse the darkness."

Chinese Proverb

We had just finished a training session in Coimbatore and were driving back as a team.

Having heard my earlier Ulundurpet story, the choice was obvious. We pulled over at the same restaurant for an evening coffee break.

As we walked in, our eyes instinctively searched for the service maestro.

He wasn't there.

We settled at a table, the tiredness of the drive was beginning to show on everyone's faces, and the expectation of a hot snack and coffee after a long training day had quietly built up in all of us. A waiter approached with a flat, mechanical greeting.

"Only coffee is available now. No evening snacks," he said.

No apology. No effort.

We tried asking if anything could be arranged.

"Only after 3.30pm. Now we don't have snacks," he replied, shutting the conversation down.

No offer to check. No willingness to help. Just a rule, delivered with finality.

Disappointed, we decided to leave and find another place.

As we stood up to leave, something changed.

A young woman from the service team approached us.

"How may I help you, sir?" she asked, with genuine concern.

We explained the situation, expecting the same answer.

Instead, she said, "Please sit, sir. Let me check." It wasn't just what she said. It was the way she said it—as though our inconvenience had become her personal responsibility.

She poured water for the table and walked straight to the kitchen.

The shift in energy was immediate.

Within minutes, she returned.

"The master can prepare Mysore Bonda and Vazhakkai Bajji for you," she said, quietly pleased.

And just like that, the problem was solved.

When the hot bondas arrived at the table, the mood changed instantly. The same group that was irritated five minutes earlier was now laughing over coffee

Curious, I asked her, "What made you come to us when we were leaving?"

"You looked disappointed," she said simply. "So, I wanted to check."

"And how did you convince the kitchen when your colleague was so sure it wasn't possible?"

She smiled. "We are here to serve what you want. I just requested the master."

That was it.

No big theory. No process. No escalation. Just intent.

In that moment, the difference was clear.

One person saw his job as enforcing rules.
The other saw it as solving a problem.

Same place. Same kitchen. Same constraints.

Different mindset.

What struck me most wasn't just that she fixed the issue.

She changed the outcome entirely.

Without her, we would have walked out and probably never returned.

Because of her, we stayed—and remembered.

As we drove away, this became the conversation in the car.

We often design complex service recovery systems—scripts, approvals, escalation matrices.

But sometimes, recovery is far simpler.

Notice the disappointment.
Take ownership.
Do something about it.

She didn't wait for permission.
She didn't follow a script.
She just cared enough to act.

And that made all the difference.

What you tolerate becomes your standard.

CHAPTER 05

The Mumbai Shopkeeper Who Upped His Shutter and His Game

"A bit of fragrance always clings to the hand that gives roses."

Chinese Proverb

I was in Mumbai for a meeting that didn't go as planned. It got pushed to the next day. I had carried only one set of clothes. Not ideal.

At around 9 p.m., the person I was meeting called. "I'll arrange a car. Go pick up what you need." Sounded simple. Until we reached the market at 11:30 p.m. Everything was shut. The streets had that late-night Mumbai stillness—shutters down, stray dogs wandering lazily, and the occasional taxi cutting through the silence

The driver stepped out to check if anything was still open. A small shop nearby was just closing. The owner had finished his aarti and was pulling down the shutter. He saw us approach. "Kya chahiye?" he asked. I explained my situation. He didn't hesitate. He lifted the shutter back up, that metallic sound of the shutter rolling upward felt strangely reassuring in that moment, he switched on the lights, and said: "Aaiye. Dekhiye."

Inside, he showed me everything—shirts, trousers, combinations—helping me choose what would work for a business meeting.

No rush. No irritation. Just intent to help. Twenty minutes later, I had everything I needed.

As he packed the clothes, I said, "I didn't expect to find anything open at this hour." He smiled. "This is Mumbai - no worries." It was a simple line. But it carried weight. In that moment, he wasn't just a shopkeeper, he was representing his city. It reminded me that sometimes entire cities build their reputation through ordinary people doing extraordinary little things.

He could have easily refused. His day was done. He was heading home. Instead, he chose to reopen. That one decision turned a transaction into a story I've told for years now.

From a business perspective, it was brilliant. One late-night sale – and hundreds of conversations that followed.

Great service doesn't always come from big gestures.

Sometimes, it's just about recognising when someone needs help—and deciding to show up.

CHAPTER 06

Spilled Drinks and Mopped Up Goodwill

"Your best customers are your greatest source of learning."

Bill Gates

Qwiky's Coffee Pub was a small 900 sqft shop tucked away in a corner of Nungambakkam. The stories we brewed there were more aromatic and powerful than the amazing coffees we served way back in the early 2000s. One such story stands out in my memory as a perfect example of how handling mistakes can create customers for life.

We had just concluded our weekly team meeting where we had reinforced our policy that we would replace drinks if spilled by a guest, whether through their mistake or by some accident. It was one of those policies that sound simple enough when discussed in a meeting room, but its real value would only be revealed when tested in the chaotic reality of a busy café.

That test came sooner than expected. A Saturday afternoon brought in the usual weekend crowd, families, college students, and professionals seeking respite from Chennai's heat. Among them was a family of four, with a bright-eyed girl of about twelve who volunteered to collect their order from the pickup counter.

She approached with determination, clearly wanting to show her parents she could handle this responsibility. Our Courtesy Crew member, the junior-most position responsible for maintaining the cleanliness of the café and furniture, noticed her approaching and helped with the heavily laden tray containing four elaborate coffee creations.

"I can do it myself," she insisted politely, her chin raised with confidence.

The crew member stepped back with an encouraging smile but stayed close as the girl lifted the tray and began her journey back to her family's table. She navigated the maze of chairs and tables with the concentration of someone transporting precious cargo. Just a few steps from her table, it happened, a slight wobble, an overcorrection, and suddenly the tray tipped.

Four perfectly made drinks turned into a cascading waterfall, splashing across the floor, nearby patrons, and worst of all, covering the small child in coffee and cream. Time seemed to slow. For a split second, the entire café froze in collective sympathy. The girl's face fell in embarrassment. She looked as though she wanted the floor to open and swallow her up.

That's when our hero stepped in, the same Courtesy Crew member who had earlier volunteered assistance. He moved with quiet efficiency, without fanfare or fluster. First, he led the ashamed and obviously agitated family to a nearby clean table: his calm and reassuring manner made them follow without question.

"These things happen all the time," he winked conspiratorially at the small child, and somehow, the way he said it made everyone around believe it.

He had hand signalled the counter staff for replacement drinks, while seating them. A new order was already under preparation by the time the family settled. He rapidly cleaned the spill, making sure nearby patrons had fresh napkins and sincere apologies.

Most remarkably, he managed to do all this while maintaining a constant stream of happy conversation with the young daughter, turning her moment of public humiliation into a lighthearted accident that might happen to anyone, including staff. The girl was laughing, the family was at ease, and what could have been a ruined trip had turned into a treasured memory by the time replacement drinks arrived at their table.

When the family eventually left, they stopped by the counter specifically to express their gratitude. The father pulled me aside and said, "We'll be coming back here often. Not just because the coffee is good, but because of how you treated us today. That's rare." His gratitude wasn't about coffee. It was about dignity

What struck me later, as I reflected on this incident, was how our crew members had gone beyond simply following policy. Yes, we had a rule about replacing spilled drinks, but the way he executed it, with empathy, efficiency, and genuine warmth, transformed a routine service recovery into a moment of connection and loyalty-building.

We built customer loyalty at Qwiky's Coffee Pub brick by brick, person by person, family by family. This incident, simple as it was, demonstrated something powerful: customers often don't remember what you said or even what you did, but they always remember how you made them feel.

By turning a moment of embarrassment into one of relief and even joy, our Courtesy-Crew member had created the kind of emotional connection that marketing budgets can't buy.

In the years that followed, that family became regular customers, often requesting "the same table where we spilled everything that time, transforming what could have been a deterrent to return into a fond tradition. All because one team member understood that service recovery isn't just about fixing mistakes, it's about making people feel valued, even and especially when things go wrong.

Customers don't see effort—they experience outcomes.

CHAPTER 07

Nafeez Latte Story

"There are no strangers here; only friends you haven't yet recognized."

William Butler Yeats

Another Qwiky's Coffee Pub tale is one where we created significant personal impacts that kept people returning. Among our vibrant group of patrons, one stands out very clearly in my memory: Nafeez.

One quiet afternoon, a young man walked into our air-conditioned café, as the Chennai sun mercilessly hammered down. He walked up to the counter with the assurance of someone who precisely knew what he wanted. He had the quiet confidence of someone who had already decided exactly how his evening would taste.

He asked for a customized latte with a double shot of doppio. Our barista looked up with a raised eyebrow. We exchanged amused glances behind the counter. This was not a routine order by any stretch. Even experienced coffee drinkers hardly ordered for a doppio, (an intensely bitter concentrated espresso shot). And here was someone asking for a double doppio

"Just to be sure - you want a double doppio?" Our barista warned, "even a single shot is quite bitter."

Nafeez, as we would know him, grinned with quiet assurance. "Just make it for me."

The barista shrugged and obliged, drawing two strong shots into his latte. We watched inquisitively as Nafeez sipped his first. His face turned from the grimace we had anticipated to show delight. He drank it as if it were a magic potion, only he understood, gave a basic "thank you," and left us perplexed and fascinated. Our barista kept staring in disbelief, almost offended that someone could enjoy something that bitter so peacefully."

Unbelievably, he came back the next day. Our barista met him this time with familiarity.

"Shall we give you the same drink as yesterday, again? double doppio lattes?"

Nafeez nodded and added quietly with pride, "Every time I come, that's the drink I want."

That instant an idea took shape. Why not respect this unusual client's signature drink if it defied accepted wisdom about coffee? Why not have fun celebrating it?

With a theatrical flourish, our barista said, "That's one 'Nafeez Latte' coming up."

Hearing his name, his eyes grew wide, and he started to smile knowing his unusual taste had just been highlighted on our unofficial menu. For a moment, he looked less like a customer and more like someone who had just found his place.

Every day Nafeez walked through our doors, our staff would call out excitedly, "One Nafeez Latte coming up!" The simple ritual turned an ordinary transaction into a personalised experience that made him feel the coffee shop equivalent of a celebrity.

Did he love it? Absolutely!! He seemed incredibly proud when his customized drink was revealed. But the next development was even more amazing.

Nafeez started inviting colleagues, classmates, even a couple of dates. "They have a drink named after me here," he said with hardly restrained enthusiasm. Every single time he said it, you could hear the pride in his voice."

Curiosity drove his friends to inevitably try the very bitter mixture, and their responses ranged from amused grimaces to impressed nods.

Ordering "the Nafeez latte" on returning visits, some even developed a taste for it. Every café has regulars. Very few have customers who accidentally become part of the culture."

What began as a simple acknowledgement of a customer's unique preference, had evolved into a marketing phenomenon costing nothing but producing strong returns. From Nafeez's regular visits as well as from the network of new patrons he brought to our café, the cash register rang steadily.

This encounter gave us some very insightful knowledge about customer personalisation. To make consumers feel unique, we did not need complex algorithms or costly CRM systems. Sometimes all it took was realizing their individuality and then reflecting it back to them in a way that would make them visible and valuable.

Though it never showed up on our printed menu, the Nafeez Latte became one of our most discussed items. It produced a chain reaction of word-of-mouth advertising that was not possible with any commercial. All because we decided to honour a customer's unusual inclination.

Years later, I frequently tell the Nafeez Latte tale when asked about customer loyalty policies. People want recognition, a sense of belonging, and the occasional thrill of hearing their name called out with a smile; they do not just want goods or services.

The human touch of personalizing becomes not only a nice-to-have but also a strong differentiator in the world of mass production and automated service of today. And occasionally, regardless of how unusual it might be, that personalization can be as basic as noting a customer's name on their preferred order.

Without realizing it, Nafeez had stopped being just another customer. He had become part of the café's folklore

Preparation is invisible—but its impact is not.

CHAPTER 08

Nirankari Baba Doppio Story

"The quiet person has the loudest mind."

African Proverb

Yet another Qwiky's Coffee Pub story unfolded with a most unexpected protagonist: a Nirankari Baba from a nearby gurdwara. In a café frequented by college students and young professionals, the sight of this spiritual figure in traditional attire certainly stood out among our diverse clientele.

It was a quiet evening when he first visited us. The rush hour had subsided, the café had settled into that rare peaceful lull between chaos and closing time and only a handful of customers remained, creating a peaceful atmosphere perfect for contemplation.

The Baba approached the counter with gentle steps, his serene presence immediately noticeable. The noise of the café somehow felt softer around him. There was an unusual calmness about him that made even busy people slow down unconsciously

"Doppio milega?" he asked in a soft voice, requesting a double espresso shot.

Our barista did a double take. Handling many customers who were not familiar with coffee terminology, this came as a pleasant surprise. Most of our first-time visitors, especially those who appeared traditional, typically needed guidance through our menu. But here was this spiritual leader, casually dropping coffee lingo with the ease of a seasoned barista.

Out of habit, our staff began explaining what a doppio was, a shot of concentrated espresso with no milk or water added, just to ensure he understood what he was ordering.

The Baba quietly waved away the explanation with a gentle hand gesture and a knowing smile. "Get me one," he said simply.

As our barista prepared the intense espresso shots, we couldn't help but wonder about this unusual customer. When his doppio was ready, the Baba received it with a slight nod, found a quiet corner, and sipped his coffee slowly, eyes half-closed in what appeared to be a meditative state. Not hurriedly. Not distractedly. Just fully present.

It looked less like someone drinking coffee and more like someone pausing life for a few peaceful minutes No phone, no book, no companion, just a man and his coffee in perfect harmony.

He finished, returned his cup to the counter with a calm smile, nodded in thanks, and left as silently as he had arrived.

To our surprise, he came back the following evening and the next; soon he became a regular feature of our café like the artwork on our walls. His schedule never changed: he would enter silently, ask for his doppio with few words, savour it alone, and leave with the same calm smile.

This turned out to be the start of a wonderful, long-lasting relationship built not on conversation but on mutual respect and understanding. Not much talk, just a pleasant smile, no order placed verbally after the first few visits as we came to anticipate his arrival, order executed precisely as he preferred, enjoyed peacefully, and another smile on exit.

Soon, our staff began referring to the intense double shot espresso as "Baba Doppio" among themselves (The name was used affectionately and with deep respect). The name stuck, and though we never officially added it to our menu, regular customers who witnessed Baba's visits began requesting it by that name.

"I'll have what the Baba has," they would say, or more directly, "One Baba Doppio, please."

What fascinated me about this relationship was how it defied conventional customer engagement wisdom. Most business literature emphasizes conversation, gathering feedback, and building verbal rapport. Yet, here was a connection built almost entirely on silent appreciation and consistency. The Baba never asked for modifications, never complained, never engaged in small talk, and perhaps that very simplicity made the relationship even more meaningful.

What lesson did we learn from the Baba Doppio experience? Perhaps it was that authentic connections come in many forms, and sometimes the quietest customers can have the most profound impact. In a business built around noise, speed, and turnover, he reminded us that some customers come searching for peace more than products.

While we celebrated the extroverted enthusiasm of customers like Nafeez, we equally valued the serene consistency of the Baba.

In a business world that often prioritizes the loud, the demanding, and the immediately profitable, our spiritual regular reminded us of the power of quiet appreciation and the value of creating space for all types of human connection. In a café built around conversations, laughter, and noise, the Baba taught us the value of silence.

The way you respond defines the experience.

CHAPTER 09

Glow in the Dark Story

"Fix the problem, not the blame."

Japanese Proverb

This is yet another narrative from the large collection of stories gathered over years at Qwiky's Coffee Pub. Beyond our coffee and cuisine, we kept a varied collection of magazines, books, mugs, greeting cards, mementos, and other curios that would appeal to our daily patrons.

One such product in our inventory was a novelty item: a playful, glow-in-the-dark novelty product. Among our customers, it was an instant hit, they bought them for bachelorette parties, amusing presents for partners, or for themselves. The product's playful, novelty character fit exactly the young, energetic environment we developed at Qwiky's.

A woman approached the counter looking worried one afternoon during a particularly busy shift. She pointed at our merchandise display instead of ordering coffee and spoke with clear discomfort. She was not angry. She was uncomfortable—and that made the feedback even more important.

Her voice lowered, but firm, she asked, "How do you think I will come and share my size with you? Label it, provide some privacy for us! Don't sell it unlabeled and unpackaged like this."

Looking at the display, I realized her worry right away. Customers would have to handle the product and check tags to ascertain sizes, so creating an uncomfortable experience in a public café as they were stacked on an open shelf without size indicators or discreet packaging.

"You're quite right," I said. "We will correct this. I appreciate you bringing this to my attention.

She shook her head sceptically and turned away, obviously not expecting any real action on her comments, and must have heard similar promises a million times before. Clearly, she expected the feedback to disappear into the black hole where most customer suggestions go.

I reported the customer's concern when my boss showed up for his regular check-in about half an hour later. He nodded understandingly and repeated what I said: "We will fix it at the earliest." With that I assumed my job was done, I had passed on the information up the chain.

What startled me next? Two hours later, I saw our boss's driver stride into the café. He headed straight to the merchandise shelf, gathered the whole supply of the product, and left without a word of explanation. Curious but preoccupied with the afternoon rush, I just mentally noted something was being done.

In barely thirty minutes, a surprisingly short time, the driver came back carrying the whole inventory. To my surprise, every object had been carefully arranged in individual, elegant boxes with outside clear size labels. There was no need to open or handle the product to check the size; no embarrassing situations at the counter; the entire shopping experience had been changed.

Now more like a boutique display than a casual merchandise corner, we stacked the recently packaged goods on the shelf.

That evening at around seven o'clock, the same lady who had expressed the concern earlier came back to the café this time accompanied by friends. She clearly double-turned as they passed the section on goods, stopping midway through to fix on the changed display.

"This is amazing!" she said, pointing out to her friends the changes. "You rock! It's amazing you corrected it so fast!" Her excitement spread faster than any marketing campaign we could have paid for.

Nearby tables turned to see what the buzz was about her shriek of incredulity and delight. Several other patrons wandered over. We sold more of the recently packaged goods by night's end than we had in the whole previous week.

This little incident highlighted something strong about customer service that transcends accepted scripts and processes.

Usually, the approach would have been to record the comments, maybe incorporate them into the next inventory planning conference, and, if possible, apply changes weeks later. Rather, our boss saw a chance to show extraordinary responsiveness.

The speed of implementation made it abundantly evident that we valued comments enough to act right away. We were not only listening to them. And the completeness of the solution, not only adding size labels but also designing appropriate packaging that improved customer experience and the perceived value of the product, showed a commitment to excellence rather than only compliance.

As I mentioned before, we developed Qwiky's Coffee Pub's reputation interaction by interaction. This narrative became yet another chapter in our unofficial customer service manual, a reminder that great companies set themselves apart from the merely good by bridging the gap between feedback and action.

Our sales of the product rose noticeably in the next weeks. Originally complaining, the lady started to regularly visit and regularly brought in new friends. Often pointing to the exhibit, she would say, “This is what I was telling you, they actually listen to their customers here.”

There is no marketing campaign that could have purchased the goodwill produced by that basic, responsive behaviour.

It’s not the problem that defines you—it’s your response to it.

CHAPTER 10

The Shop-In-Shop Turnaround Story

"If you want to go fast, go alone. If you want to go far, go together."

African Proverb

Talking about Qwiky's Coffee Pub – I could speak about it endlessly. It was one of those organisations that had a huge impact on many of us who were building our careers in those days. The lessons learnt there continue to shape my approach to business even now. Here is one professional story that stands out in my memory.

The Music World store in Spencer Plaza was a happening place in Chennai back then. Many youngsters used to hang around there, browsing through CDs and cassettes, soaking in the latest music trends. The management decided to start a café within the store to capitalize on this foot traffic, and they were doing a decent job of it.

Then one of their executives suggested – why not bring in experts to take their in-store café to the next level? They approached Qwiky's, already known for our coffee expertise and vibrant atmosphere. After a series of meetings, we decided to partner with them. The shop-in-shop café was handed over to us, the "experts."

What happened next was both unexpected and humbling at once. Within two weeks of taking over, our sales had nosedived, and we were performing poorly. The excitement of the partnership had quickly turned into anxiety and uncomfortable review meetings.

The Music World management was puzzled, and internally, as often happens when results don't materialize, a few heads were expected to roll. The pressure was immense – this was supposed to be our expertise, yet we were performing worse than the original setup.

We called an emergency meeting to address this alarming situation. One good thing about the culture we had fostered at Qwiky's was that there was no fear to speak up, regardless of your position in the hierarchy. Ideas were valued more than designations.

And speak up one newcomer did. A young man who had joined us just a few months earlier raised his hand confidently, amidst the tense atmosphere. "Give it to me - I'll turn it around." He spoke with the dangerous confidence only newcomers and visionaries usually possess

His confidence was infectious but at the same time unsettled many of us seniors. The unspoken thought hung in the air – what we could not achieve as a team with years of experience, how would this newbie manage on his own?

I looked at him skeptically. "If I give the store to you, what exactly will you do?"

Without hesitation, he said, "Increase sales threefold."

"How?" I pressed, not convinced.

He said he had plans and he had some conditions – he wanted to introduce smaller bite-sized snacks and smaller versions of our drinks. But his most unusual request was for a caramel popcorn machine – something uncommon in cafés at the time and costing approximately around ₹20,000. With no revenue coming in and our reputation at stake, this was a significant risk.

Nonetheless, adhering to our "no fear" policy, I went and asked for permission from my bosses. They immediately asked the question I wasn't prepared for: "When will the money come back? What's the ROI?"

I heard the term Return on Investment for the first ever time in my life and, without much calculation, I blurted out, "Three weeks."

My boss laughed and said, "Are you joking? How is that even possible? Even if you give it back over three months, it's fine." With that, permission was granted.

What happened next was nothing short of magic. Our sales jumped eightfold instead of just threefold within the first week of using the newcomer's ideas! Across the music store, the smell of freshly made caramel popcorn was irresistible to browsing patrons. Customers who had walked in casually now slowed down instinctively, trying to locate where the irresistible aroma was coming from. The smaller, more reasonably priced snacks and beverages let people enjoy a quick treat without committing themselves to a full meal or big drink.

The turnaround was complete – our reputation was restored, business boomed, and the stock value of all those who had their jobs on the line skyrocketed! The same people who had quietly doubted the idea were now enthusiastically discussing expansion possibilities. The young newcomer became something of a legend within our organisation.

What struck me most about this experience was not just the impressive sales figures, but the powerful lesson about trust and innovation. We could have easily dismissed the newcomer's ideas based on his lack of experience. We could have played it safe with conventional approaches that weren't working but wouldn't risk additional investment.

Instead, by creating a culture where even the newest team member felt empowered to speak up, and by being willing to take a calculated risk on a fresh perspective, we discovered a solution that none of the "experts" had considered.

How trust and good practises help us take leaps of faith in life and at work is something that has to be experienced to be believed. This incident fundamentally shaped my understanding of leadership – sometimes, the best thing a leader can do is to get out of the way and trust those with fresh eyes to see solutions invisible to the experienced.

The young man went on to become one of our most innovative team members, and the caramel popcorn became a signature offering across many of our locations. The Music World café turned into one of our most profitable outlets, proving that expertise isn't just about what you know, but about your willingness to recognize good ideas regardless of their source.

Sometimes innovation is not about inventing something revolutionary. It is about noticing human behaviour more accurately than everyone else

Sometimes, the simplest idea creates the biggest turnaround.

CHAPTER 11

The Café Turnaround Story

"Every sale begins with a conversation" –

Unknown

Yet another Qwiky's story, don't worry - it is not over yet! After the immense runaway success of the first store, as it happens often, we opened a bigger, better outlet about 3 kilometres away from the original location. Naturally, people tend to compare the newer sibling with the earlier successful one. I was entrusted with the responsibility of running the show there, perhaps as recognition for the job done at the first store.

Despite the promising location and heightened expectations, the dream start did not materialize. Even with an all-Hotel Management educated team and experienced managers, we performed poorly, averaging just ₹8,000 a day in sales. Every evening closing felt heavier than the previous one. This dismal performance continued for about three months.

Then came the day I had been dreading. During our review meeting, the boss delivered the news- it hit like a thunderbolt: they were going to inform the landlord about the termination of the lease agreement as we weren't meeting expectations. The break-even point for the store was ₹16,000 daily, and we were nowhere close. We weren't just fighting poor sales anymore.

We were fighting for survival. We had about 17 days left in the month before the notice would be served.

Those days, it wasn't easy to get jobs as opportunities were scarce. After being let go for poor performance, your employability would have taken a serious hit. We met as a team, facing a massive challenge as a team, it meant the end of the road for most of us, in fact, all of us.

We brainstormed intensely, grasping for solutions. While we were deep in discussion, an insurance salesman, a friend of mine who happened to be at the store, was overhearing our conversation. He asked if he could butt in, and we readily agreed, as we weren't making any headway.

Then he dropped a bombshell: "You're not engaging with customers, and that's why your sales are low!"

His comment felt like a blow below the belt. Here we were, a bunch of dedicated souls slogging our backsides off and, in our minds, doing a very good job on customer service. It was a bitter pill to accept, let alone swallow. He held his ground as we demanded evidence, and the discussion grew heated and extended.

Finally, reluctantly, we decided to put his suggestion to work. We divided responsibilities strategically:

The cashier would take on the job of persuading customers who came for coffee to try something to eat. (It was our natural assumption that customers knew best and needed no suggestions. We thought, "Won't they think we're being pushy? They know what they want, right?"

We couldn't have been more wrong! That realization changed the way many of us would approach customers for the rest of our careers. We were very happy to be proved wrong.

One team member who was particularly good with children took responsibility for entertaining the kids. We had noticed that parents who came with children were often unable to enjoy their orders and almost invariably had to leave in a rush as their children grew restless.

Another person took responsibility for actively selling merchandise instead of just having it on display.

To cut a long story short, our sales jumped from ₹8,000 to ₹16,000 in just three days. The energy in the café transformed almost overnight. The same space suddenly felt alive. We were thrilled! We rushed to our boss and shared this news with great glee, requesting him to reconsider cancelling the lease.

We were met with a very cold matter of fact response: "So what happened to all these days' sales? Who will give me the difference amount?" Somewhat disappointed but still hopeful, we returned to the café with renewed enthusiasm and set about our task of increasing sales further. The new magic potion we had discovered, active engagement with customers, was taking massive hold on us. We succeeded, satisfying both our customers and boosting profits.

The CEO of a company that was clearing Chennai of its solid waste was one of our regular customers. He used to order a sandwich and coffee for his lunch, which added up to ₹180.

When we got to talk with him, we discovered that his lunch allowance was ₹1,000 (he was an expatriate), and he was eating at the neighbouring star hotel which used to set him back by ₹800 before shifting partially to our place. And like many customers, he had needs we would never have discovered if we had stayed transactional

Then we saw an opportunity for a "win-win" situation. We suggested chips, dessert, a drink to wash it down, and a book to read during and after lunch. His bill grew to ₹400, still well below his allowance, while substantially increasing our sales.

Parents who came with their children would find themselves suddenly free to enjoy their coffee as our "child expert" took charge, engaging the kids with teddy bears and fun activities. And voilà! When the children left, they often had one or two teddy bear "friends" firmly clutched in their arms. The father and child would negotiate and typically end up purchasing one teddy bear for ₹500, further boosting our sales. Were the father and child unhappy? Not at all. Were we unhappy? Not at all!

A famous actress visited one day, having heard about our brownie with ice cream, which was a novelty back then. She ordered six brownies, adding ₹900 to our top line. She returned for the next two days and then stopped coming. We had her number and took the liberty to call her. She explained that everything was nice, but the ice cream was melting by the time she got home, if we could find a solution, she would come back.

That very night at 9:30, we called the ice cream vendor (how could he sleep when we were building sales?!) and explained the problem. There was a solution: a cello thermal container that could maintain temperature long enough for us to deliver ice cream that wouldn't melt. "Give me three," I told the vendor. When he asked why three, I replied, "One with the customer, one in store, and one with us for next day's delivery." That's how we retained that valuable customer.

Many such stories resulted in our taking the sales up to ₹64,000 per day, an eightfold increase!! If anyone had suggested even a two-fold increase before we discovered the joy of proactive selling, it would have seemed to us that either they were out of their mind or they were complete idiots!

This story didn't end there. All of us carried this experience into our next jobs, making ourselves proud and our new employers happy.

We had spent months waiting for customers to buy. The breakthrough came only when we started helping them discover.

Success is very infectious, indeed very, very infectious!
Sales don't grow by chance—they grow by conversation.

CHAPTER 12

The Y2K Cracker Story

"Life is ten percent what happens and ninety percent how you react."

Japanese Proverb

Though it is more of a comic relief from all the "MORE" stories, this narrative also offers a little lesson. Everyone was caught up in the Y2K frenzy as the turn of the millennium drew near, some worried about computer apocalypse, others just eager to mark a once-in-a-lifetime calendar event.

We at Qwiky's decided to maximize this historical event. Complete with MTV VJs, local celebrities, and a huge countdown scheduled for our guests, we had set up an extravagant New Year's Eve celebration Months of preparation had gone into this event, special millennium-themed menus, mementos, and an amazing fireworks show to greet Y2K with suitable fanfare.

The evening started wonderfully. The café buzzed with the nervous excitement of people waiting to witness history together. Our café became a humming celebration area full of eager patrons wearing their best. There was a charged expectation in the air. The crowd got more animated as midnight drew near.

With a microphone in hand, the MTV VJ started the last countdown. "Ten!" The crowd yelled.

Nine" The volume climbed with every count. "Eight!" People lifted their glasses.

"Seven! The moment was ready for cameras to record. Six! The excitement was palpable.

Five Everybody was concentrating on the countdown.

"Four!" - and the crackers went off, shocking and confusing everyone. For two full seconds, nobody knew whether to celebrate or panic

Looking at each other with expressions ranging from uncertainty to incredulity, both the audience and we, the organisers, were momentarily left in stunned quiet. Had we count backwards instead of forwards? Had someone jumped the gun? This early celebration broke the well calibrated moment.

Then we knew what had happened as the first uncertainty cleared. Our great excitement to coordinate the ideal front-of-house experience had left the other end of our fireworks arrangement totally neglected. Seeing a chance to ring in Y2K in grand style, an over-enthusiastic bystander chose to light the other end of our meticulously planned fireworks show with his beedi, so adding to the celebrations. In his mind, he was probably helping us create a bigger celebration.

Originally meant to be a dramatic crescendo at "Happy New Year!" "Four!" had become an absurd anticlimactic ending.

Laughter spread through the crowd following the first shock. With amazing clarity of mind, the MTV VJ quipped, "Well, I guess even our fireworks couldn't wait for Y2K!" This totally released stress, and shortly everyone was laughing wildly.

Though without the planned pyrotechnic climax, the countdown started again. And somehow, the second attempt felt even more joyful because everyone was now laughing together.

When midnight finally arrived, the celebration was no less festive, perhaps even more real given the surprising, unexpected twist.

The next day, as we were tidying up and talking about the evening's events, I realized how this accident had turned out to be the most unforgettable part of the evening. What could have been a catastrophe had turned into a tale consumers were already delightedly remembering? Many people said that the jumble of the celebrations was quite fitting following months of Y2K stress and preparation.

Still, the event was a sobering reminder of a fundamental business lesson: you need to have all ends covered- quite literally, when planning activities, promotions, or any client experience. It's not enough to concentrate on the most obvious aspects; occasionally, the overlooked details can take over your carefully thought-out plans.

For all later events at Qwiky's, we adopted a more all-encompassing strategy for planning, assigning team members to oversee every facet of the event, not only the glitzy front-end operations. Though we laughed about the Y2K cracker episode for years, we also grew from it.

In the big picture, our early fireworks show was not really important. Beyond a brief disturbance of timing, no damage was done; it gave our clients a unique narrative about how they embraced the new millennium. In business, though, not all such mistakes have such benign results. Sometimes the neglected "other end" is a crucial component causing otherwise outstanding performance to suffer.

This became one of our guiding ideas as we entered the new millennium:

The evening taught us that customers forgive imperfect execution surprisingly fast when the emotion remains intact

Excellence is about making sure even the elements consumers do not see are managed with the same care and attention, not only about doing the obvious things right.

CHAPTER 13

The Q-4 Cost Cutting Project

"Necessity is the mother of invention."

Plato

Here's another Qwiky's Coffee Pub story. Building that organisation became a real-world lesson in business administration for all of us. The lessons learnt during those formative years continue to shape my approach to business challenges even today.

This story revolves around our fourth store. The first store, with just 900 square feet, had required a significant investment by the standards of the time. For context, this was before entrepreneurship was glamorized and before capital was easily accessible.

When we were planning to build our fourth store, there was an important addition to the leadership team, an early IIT alumnus with a strong sense of financial discipline. The way he got to the nitty-gritty of costs was a valuable life lesson.

Luckily, I volunteered for what seemed like a tortuous journey. (In those days, working with demanding bosses was called "torture", though in retrospect, these experiences were the most formative.)

Our target was ambitious and seemed nearly impossible: to build a store that was 2,000 square feet, more than twice the size of our original location, but at a budget of just ₹24 lakhs, including all equipment.

Almost everyone gave up even before we started. The project had already been declared impossible before the first nail was purchased. The chorus of negative voices was overwhelming:

"Impossible"

"Brand standards will get diluted." "You're setting yourself up for failure."

Doom-sayers and nay-sayers held sway throughout the organisation. I found myself caught in a whirlpool of doubt. It's amazing how quickly negativity spreads inside organizations.

Had I made the right decision by volunteering? Was I attaching my name to an inevitable failure?

But the IIT graduate was unfazed by the negativity swirling around the project. One day, noticing my hesitation, he asked directly if I wanted to quit his team. His steely determination struck a totally different chord with me. He didn't speak like someone trying to survive the project. He spoke like someone determined to redefine it. Instead of being intimidated, I found myself inspired. I decided to stick my neck out, and what a decision it turned out to be - absolute gold!

His approach was methodical and eye-opening. For example, we had been buying chairs from a company for ₹ 1,800 per piece. He called a local fabricator and said, "Take a look at what goes into this chair, break it down and give me a material estimate".

This was the first time I heard that approach, and it was the first of many such firsts. And once you begin questioning assumptions, it becomes difficult to stop.

Every single item on the equipment list, furniture list, and fixture list was put to such scrutiny. Nothing was taken at face value; everything was questioned, broken down to its components, and evaluated for necessity and value.

In summary, the results (to spare you the excessive details) were remarkable:

A chair that cost us ₹1,800 was replicated by a fabricator and upholsterer at ₹250. We bought nails by kilograms for the project rather than in pre-packaged quantities. We eliminated one chest freezer and a vertical refrigerator by reengineering our production processes

Most importantly, we studied each element of the café experience to determine what truly mattered to customers and what was merely tradition or assumption on our part.

We pulled off the project at the target budget of ₹24 lakhs. And the most astounding part? Nobody noticed anything different, not the customers, not the staff, not the nay-sayers and doomsayers, not even the press when they came to cover our newest location. That was the real victory—cost had reduced, but experience had not. The customer experience remained intact, and by all metrics, the store was as successful as our other previous locations.

The money saved was roughly around ₹1.25 crores compared to what it would have cost using our previous approaches, a staggering amount at that time.

But the lessons learnt were invaluable and stay with us still:

- Question assumptions about what things "should" cost
- Break down complex items to their components to understand true value
- Engineer processes around outcomes rather than traditions
- Don't accept industry standards without scrutiny
- Focus resources on what matters to customers

This experience fundamentally changed how I approach business challenges. I learnt that "impossible" often simply means "hasn't been done yet," and that constraints can drive innovation rather than limit it.

I'm sharing this story so that we all might learn and use these principles somewhere in our lives. Whether you're building a business, managing a department, or simply trying to stretch your personal budget, the approach remains powerful: question, analyze, reimagine, and optimize with focus on what truly delivers value.

We learnt that customers rarely pay for internal complexity. They pay for perceived value.

Efficiency is not about cutting cost—it's about removing waste.

CHAPTER 14

The Hotel Lobby Accommodation That Turned Out to Be a Blessing

"A visitor is a blessing."

African Proverb

Let's step away from the Qwiky's Coffee Pub stories for a moment. This one goes somewhat earlier; I was working in a hotel at that time. During the quieter hours, when most guests were already in their rooms and the busy check-in activity had stopped one night, I was the duty manager. The hotel had settled into that strange midnight quiet, known only to hospitality professionals. A well-dressed but obviously hassled man entered our lobby about 12:30 am.

His manner suggested urgency, but he carried himself with the trained grace of someone used to business travel. But exhaustion had clearly overtaken professionalism. He addressed the front desk straight and without any preamble.

"Look, I need a place to rest. Even the lobby is good enough for me," he said. "I have to get fresh, get ready, and head out by 4:30 am. I will need fresh towels and coffee.

Though clearly tired, he looked elegant and professional. "None of the hotels with which I regularly do business were able to assist me with a room or provide any alternatives, which is why I am here," he stated following a brief stop.

I found myself in a dilemma. Hotel procedures were clear-cut on one hand; lobbies were not for sleeping and letting non-guests use facilities could lead to problems. On the other hand, this felt different somehow. Whether it was hospitality intuition, a refined sense of salesmanship, or just a want to assist a human being in his hour of need, I didn't know what motivated me, but I felt compelled to help him. Sometimes experience teaches you that a guest's urgency matters more than the rulebook.

Already thinking of a solution, I said, "Sir, let me see what I can arrange for you."

I arranged a spot for him in the lobby, separating one of our cozier sofas with some decorative screens to offer privacy. I set up a comfortable spot for him to relax, offered a fresh towel as asked, and guided him to the executive locker room so he could clean-up. I made sure his 4:30 a.m. coffee would be ready before he arrived.

It was a significant risk; indeed, I was far too junior to make such unusual choices. Should something go wrong or if top management learnt about this arrangement, I would almost certainly face tough questions. But something about this called for transcending accepted practices.

For those several hours, the gentleman slept peacefully. He was awake and savoring his coffee after freshening up at 4:30 am sharp as promised.

He seemed grateful for the temporary lodging as he got ready to go. It was the gratitude of someone who had spent hours being turned away.

He turned over his visiting card as he left, and I was staring at the Station Director of Air India's credentials! As I came to see the possible importance of this meeting, my heart skipped a beat. In hospitality, you never truly know who is standing in front of you—or what one act of kindness, may eventually become. For more than four years, they had not given our hotel any business because of some unresolved conflict or communication breakdown.

"Where every seasoned hotel professional failed me, you just didn't ask who I am and gave me what I wanted," he said, smiling. "I know your hotel hasn't been getting any Air India business for the last four years; I'm going to correct that situation today."

As promised, we later that same day got 26 rooms from Air India layoff passengers. By the end of the shift, we had sold 127 rooms out of our 117-room hotel, where 16 rooms were under repair and blocked! This meant innovative ideas, crew members' room sharing, and some quick thinking by our whole staff.

The sales manager, who also oversaw me, drew me aside with a confused look the next day. "Tere ko Maths aata hai kya?" he asked. "How can you sell 127 rooms in a 101-room hotel?"

The answer was straightforward but significant: anything is possible when genuine hospitality takes over. Apparently unachievable magic numbers just fall into your lap when you pay more attention to human needs than to strict guidelines.

This encounter strengthened a principle I have carried with me throughout my career: business success often results from identifying human events that demand exceptions rather than from following rules. That night the Station Director needed rest, cleanliness, and punctuality, basic needs all the protocol-bound hotels had failed to meet. He did not need luxury.

My record of notching high "numbers" at companies that I had worked for, had one more addition, but more importantly, I came to know what hospitality means. It's about responding to what the guest needs, even if, perhaps especially, that need falls outside of standard offerings; it's not about providing what's handy for the company.

That night, we didn't sell a room. We delivered relief

Outstanding service begins the moment rigid rules are put aside.

CHAPTER 15

Ramesh: The One Who Doesn't Hear "No" At Shell

"The person who says it cannot be done should not interrupt the person doing it."

Chinese Proverb

Yet another company that brings non-stop nostalgia and innumerable stories is my stint at Shell. We were building our first team, and the Shell leadership told me that I had to recruit a minimum of three differently abled people at my site. I had no choice but to follow the mandate, though I wasn't particularly enthusiastic about it.

We went to a Differently Abled Persons (DAP) job mela conducted by Ability Foundation. There, I met a young man named Ramesh, a person with hearing-impairment with an unmistakable spark in his eyes. He was already shortlisted by the Department of Posts, Government of India, and was there merely job shopping. He came and sat down across from me during the interview and somehow took an immediate liking to me, expressing his desire to join Shell instead.

Here was a guy willing to give up a guaranteed government job! And yet, I was not inclined to hire a person with hearing-impairment.

My mind was full of objections.: How will I communicate with him? How will he communicate with customers? With colleagues? My mind said no—and initially, so did I. Looking back now, I realize most of those limitations existed in me, not in him

But Shell put its foot down, insisting we meet our inclusion targets, and so I reluctantly added Ramesh to my team, not a happy addition for obvious reasons. The rest of the story is about how he systematically dismantled my objections and reservations, and how we built a relationship of mutual respect and growth.

We gave him what seemed like an ordinary and easy job of directing traffic at the petrol station. Six days later, I noticed complete chaos on the forecourt, customers reversing and traffic going helter-skelter. Concerned, I approached my manager to understand what was happening.

"Sir, Ramesh has his day off today!" he explained simply.

I snapped back, "So what?" not understanding the connection.

His reply was eye-opening: "Sir, he has an uncanny sense of anticipation and judgment. He just takes a quick glance, identifies where the fuel tank is positioned on each vehicle, knows which island is free or getting free soon, and directs vehicles there accordingly. No one else can manage the flow like he does."

There was something special about this young man, wake-up call number one. Ramesh was beginning to solve problems we had accepted as normal.

A few days went by, and during a briefing session, Ramesh approached me and indicated through gestures that he would like to work on the pump itself, not just direct traffic. I immediately said no way. He asked for an explanation, which I didn't provide. For the next three months, almost every day, he would make it a point to run into me and keep asking the same question through notes and gestures. After a point, I started avoiding him and sneaking into the office through alternate entrances. Persistence has a strange power—it slowly wears down certainty."

During another team meeting, he cornered me with another request. This time his note was more direct: "You have brains. Use them and find me a way of doing this."

I was in a classic bind, if I did nothing, the implication was that I had no brains, a deeply unsettling thought! He made me lose sleep pondering solutions. Because somewhere deep inside, I knew he was right. Finally, my team and I brainstormed and arrived at the idea of a communication board, a slate with stickers indicating price or volume where the customer had to tick and write either the amount or the volume they wanted. Ramesh liked the concept, we liked it, and we immediately implemented it.

Problems surfaced almost immediately. A group of about 10-15 agitated customers approached me complaining that this new system was too slow, especially during peak traffic hours. As they voiced their frustration, I could see Ramesh watching me with anxious eyes, apprehensive that his dreams of advancement would be extremely short-lived.

Those looks gave me the courage to tell the customers that they could please use all other islands except number 5, which would be Ramesh's assigned pump on days he worked. That was a significant leap of faith. The customers shook their heads in disagreement and walked away, clearly unsatisfied with my answer.

We were convinced he would find a way to win them over somehow. On the afternoon of that same day, Ramesh had gone out and bought a ₹5 scribbling pad, a ₹5 pen, and an ₹85 calculator. He had devised his own mechanism to cope with his challenge of slowness.

His solution was brilliantly simple: he would hand over the slate to customers waiting in the queue so they could fill it up while waiting. As he serviced one vehicle, he would enter details into his scribbling pad, then erase the board and give it to the next customer in line. This way, he prepared multiple orders simultaneously, dramatically increasing his efficiency. What impressed me wasn't the tool. It was the ownership."

Later, we discovered another remarkable benefit, he had no cash shortages because of this practise. He would never miss collecting payment, and he would consistently be the first to finish his settlement after each shift because he had all the transaction data meticulously recorded.

As time went on, Ramesh continued to excel. He eventually became a supervisor, applying these same systematic approaches to managing the air gauge station and the convenience store. He had found his solution and an ally in me, who had transformed from a sceptic to his advocate. By then, many of the same people who initially doubted him had begun learning from him.

This experience taught me profoundly about what sheer determination, discipline, and focus can do for ordinary individuals. It's that little extra, that refusal to accept limitations, that makes certain people extraordinary. Ramesh didn't just overcome the communication barriers; he created systems of his own that proved more effective than our standard approaches.

In the end, the mandate that I had initially resisted became one of the most valuable learning experiences of my career. Ramesh showed me that limitations often exist more in our perceptions and that with the right attitude, challenges become opportunities for innovation.

Ramesh never asked for sympathy. He asked for opportunity.

The moment you trust people, they begin to prove you right.

CHAPTER 16

Ramesh at Burger Man

"The only disability in life is a bad attitude."

Scott Hamilton

At the end of 2009, I was leaving Shell, and I conveyed the news to my team. Their reactions were mixed, some wanted to leave with me, while others opted to stay. Ramesh, however, had a different approach. He didn't want to stay, but neither did he simply resign. Instead, he asked me directly to find him an alternate job, showing the same determination that had made him such an exceptional team member.

Around that time, Burger Man was expanding its presence across Chennai, opening kiosks outside famous stores and office complexes. This new line of business presented an opportunity. Since I knew Ramesh to be an extraordinary staff member, I didn't hesitate to suggest his name to Sunil Cherian, the owner at Burger Man.

Sunil was nervous and hesitant when I first brought Ramesh up, he was exactly where I had been five years ago when first met him. I could almost hear my old doubts echoing through his questions. The same concerns surfaced: How would a person with hearing-impairment interact with patrons in a fast-food restaurant where effective, quick communication is vital? During hectic lunch rushes, how would he manage orders?

Despite his reservations, Sunil agreed to give Ramesh a one-week trial. Ramesh was assigned to the Tiruvanmiyur store, which was closest to his house, a practical consideration that would minimize his commute time.

A week later, I received a call from Sunil. My heart sank slightly as I answered, expecting to hear that he had indeed tried Ramesh out as committed, but things weren't working out. I prepared myself to look for another opportunity for him.

To my surprise and delight, Sunil had an entirely different story to tell, one that I'm delighted to share with you now.

Ramesh had joined Burger Man with the same innovative spirit he had shown at Shell. By now, he had perfected his famous communication template. On his very first day, he spent his own money creating a professional-looking sticker showing a lip and an ear crossed out in red, clearly indicating that he could neither speak nor hear. Most people wait for organizations to empower them. Ramesh empowered himself first.

Beside this visual, he prominently displayed his mobile number where customers could send SMS messages to place their orders.

This simple move turned what could have been seen as a disadvantage into a unique selling proposition. The young tech professionals working in the office buildings surrounding the kiosk didn't see a limitation—they saw innovation that aligned perfectly with their text-messaging lifestyle. To them, the SMS ordering system didn't look like a limitation. It looked ahead of its time.

Rather than seeing his responsibility as simply standing at the kiosk and waiting for customers to approach, Ramesh reimagined the entire business model. He used to actively solicit orders via text message starting from 9 AM, then begin preparing them strategically so he could deliver them efficiently to nearby offices.

He didn't wait for customers to come to him; he took Burger Man to them. He understood something fundamental about sales—convenience itself is a product.

When he was away making deliveries, another clear sign conveyed that he was out delivering orders and provided his number again so new customers could text their orders in the meantime. He tracked all incoming messages meticulously, ensuring that not a single order fell through.

The net result was nothing short of extraordinary. The Tiruvanmiyur kiosk, which had been doing a healthy average daily sale of ₹2,500 (already the highest in the network), started consistently hitting the ₹10,000 mark per day, a fourfold increase!

What had begun as a favour to help place a differently abled employee had turned into a business revelation. Ramesh hadn't just adapted to his new environment; he had transformed it entirely, creating a text-to-order system years before food delivery apps would make such approaches commonplace.

This encounter strengthened something I had discovered during my time with Ramesh at Shell: often, our perceived constraints become the very spur for creativity. Ramesh's inability to hear or speak verbally did not lessen his capacity for communication; rather, it just motivated him to find more effective outlets. His strategy enhanced customer experience, making ordering easier and increasing sales at the same time.

Sunil, who had been reluctant to gamble on Ramesh, started to support him most actively. He would often consider in our later talks how close he had come to missing out on this game-changing team member simply because of preconceptions about disability.

What is a MORE illustrative story about MORE than this? Here was someone who consistently refused to be defined by what he couldn't do, focusing instead on amplifying what he could. He didn't just meet expectations, he shattered them, converting every challenge into an opportunity to excel.

Ramesh's journey from Shell to Burger Man exemplifies the central theme of this book: it's not our circumstances that define our limits, but our willingness to go beyond them, to find the MORE that exists in every situation when we refuse to accept conventional boundaries.

Once again, Ramesh proved that extraordinary people don't merely adapt to systems. They redesign them.

When you own your difference, it becomes your edge.

CHAPTER 17

Empowerment is a System

"Give a man a fish and you feed him for a day.
Teach him how to fish and you feed him for a lifetime."

Chinese Proverb

My Shell experiences still offer rich sources of business knowledge. This narrative centers on an invention that questioned accepted wisdom in the sector and exposed striking lessons on workplace diversity and empowerment. Over the years, I realized something important—empowerment sounds inspiring in training rooms but becomes messy very quickly without clarity

Our female team members had started to show something quite amazing over the first few months following the opening of our Shell location. The stations where we had hired more women regularly displayed better productivity measures and startling sales figures. Though I hadn't yet fully understood its ramifications, gender diversity clearly correlated with business performance.

Our signature at Shell was regular staff meetings; we valued open communication and group problem-solving. One such meeting, a young woman on our team proposed an idea that first seemed simple but would later change our business process.

"Sir, what if we try assigning an all-women shift?" She suggested, her voice tinged with challenge but also confidence.

I related right away with the concept. I had heard about an all-women petrol pump in Mylapore and the amazing business goodwill it had produced during my college years. The idea had stayed with me, and here was a chance to carry out something comparable.

"That sounds like a fascinating experiment," I said. "Let us schedule it out."

The ladies on our team eagerly embraced the challenge, fast grouping themselves and choosing a Wednesday for their first shift. As the preparations went on, they came to me with an unanticipated ask.

One of them grinned mischievously and said, "Sir, since it's an all-women's shift," "you please stay away!"

Though taken aback, I valued their want to really own this project. I promised to stay away while they operated the station by themselves.

That first Wednesday brought both enthusiasm and anxiety. Although I admit to routinely checking my phone for updates or emergency calls, I maintained the promised distance. None emerged during the shift; the team managed everything perfectly.

More amazing was what followed: the experiment started methodically debunking long-held beliefs about gender roles in our sector.

Some had claimed that "women cannot handle the air gauge for an hour". Still, they handled it easily all through the shift.

The women asked, "Can we try doing a full day next time?" inspired by their success. We agreed, and they proved just as able to keep up their performance over an entire working day.

"What about decantation?" the next question the critics posed. "We are convinced they cannot manage that." Traditionally thought of as a "man's job," decantation, the process of moving gasoline from tankers into the underground tanks, was physically taxing work.

They accepted this challenge as well, finishing the process with accuracy and care to leave no frontier unbroken.

Riding this success, the team came to me with their most ambitious idea yet: "Sir, why don't we make Wednesdays a full women's day at the station?"

We successfully applied this idea for more than a year, developing a distinct character for our outlet in the process. Drawn by the first-rate service and the unique energy of the all-women team, clients started especially picking Wednesdays to visit our station.

Was this road taken without difficulty? Yes not. Day one of the initiative marked our first big test. For the women's shift, we closed an hour earlier than usual according to corporate policy. Sadly, a customer with a medical emergency arrived just after closing and needed air for his tires most urgently. Finding the station closed, he complained.

To explain the circumstances, I personally gave him a call. He at first stayed unhappy, not sure about my justification for the early closing.

"I know your new initiative," he said, "but in emergencies, what are people supposed to do?"

His question was legitimate and made us rethink our procedures. We changed our rules to keep regular hours while keeping the all-women staffing on Wednesdays.

The narrative changed course when this same client came to our station the following Wednesday. The team's first-rate performance left him, in his own words, "charmed and swept off his feet." Later, he specifically called me to applaud the initiative.

"What a wonderful idea," he said with great enthusiasm. "The service was first-rate, much above average. You are onto something quite unique here.

We remain friends until this day, and his path from critic to activist wonderfully captures the influence of this project.

Wednesdays dedicated to women produced several layers of value. It gave our female team members chances to show skills previously questioned. For our company, it produced a unique service offering that consumers particularly sought out. It questioned established ideas in society about gender roles in employment.

Most importantly, it made clear that diversity is a strong business strategy rather than only a social responsibility project. Customer loyalty and higher sales directly resulted from the fresh ideas, cooperative efforts, and service orientation our women's team brought to the operation.

The success of this program was not in proving women could perform tasks equivalent to those of men. It was about realizing that often great results come from using several approaches to the same problems. Our female team members improved rather than merely copied current procedures, adding fresh ideas and enthusiasm to all facets of the business.

The organizations that scale service excellence are rarely dependent on heroes. They build systems that allow ordinary people to consistently do extraordinary things.

Results improve when systems do.

CHAPTER 18

Oil Sale Story: How It Started

"Do not limit your challenges.
Challenge your limits."

Chinese Proverb

The year 2007 presented hitherto unheard-of difficulties for the Indian fuel retail sector. Global oil price volatility brought on by the Gulf War was being felt most strongly at our Shell station. While government-owned petrol stations kept subsidized rates, private companies like us suffered the whole weight of market forces.

The price difference was astounding at our pumps, almost ₹27 per liter more than at public sector outlets. From vantage point, that was about a 50% premium in those days. The effect was instantaneous and catastrophic. Our once-busy forecourt turned into a deserted length of concrete. Consumers would drive by, glance at our price boards, and then keep moving on without thinking twice.

Days went by with hardly any activity. Though our station remained operational despite growing losses, the mood grew progressively dark. We planned spontaneous games and events during what would typically be our busiest times to keep team morale high. These diversions helped, but they couldn't cover the basic issue: our team was designed for service, not to sit around idly.

After roughly a week of this forced inactivity, several team members came up to me clearly annoyed.

"Sir, we need actual work," one of them said quite explicitly. "We're here to serve consumers; these games are fine but, not forever."

Their commitment really spoke to me. Rather than just gathering their pay during this trying time, they wanted to help and feel generally useful. This was about pride and purpose as much as it was about covering time.

One of our brainstorming sessions that followed revealed a young team member's observation that would prove crucial.

"Sir, have you observed we have so much engine oil stock sitting unused in our storage?" he asked. "Why don't we try providing change services for motorbikes? People need that regardless of the cost of gasoline.

The recommendation hit like a flash insight. We had space, inventory, and most importantly, a motivated staff searching for meaningful work. A quick computation revealed that a basic tool and equipment investment was little, just about ₹300 for a starting kit.

Let us do it, I said right away. We gathered the required tools by the next morning and informed the staff about our new service line.

Without any official marketing, our staff members went to the street. They started approaching motorcyclists at nearby traffic signals and striking up discussions about the value of routine oil changes. Their vitality was contagious.

Though modest, the results were encouraging. Five motorbike owners gambled on our new service on day one. The next day that figure doubled to ten.

We serviced fifteen motorcycles by the third day. Though against the backdrop of our empty forecourt, these were not remarkable figures by any means but rather reflected momentum and hope. At that stage, we weren't trying to build a major sales category. We were simply trying to understand customer behaviour better.

Unexpected events cut off our little victory celebration on the evening of the third day. A company official came to see us regarding safety procedures.

"This operation isn't being conducted in a manner that meets safety criteria," he told us. "You'll need to suspend this service right now."

My heart fell. Among difficult conditions, we had discovered a ray of hope; now it was being extinguished. Returning to our former state of forced inactivity demoralized me. My team members' expressions clearly showed disappointment already.

But I resolved to keep on rather than just accepting this loss. "Sir, we understand safety is paramount," I told him. "Could you link us with the appropriate authorities to enable us to safely apply this service instead of stopping totally? We are ready to make whatever required changes."

This strategy, looking for direction instead of confronting authority, turned out successful. Seeing our sincere want to comply while still serving our community, the official agreed to assist us in negotiating the safety requirements.

We had put in place appropriate waste disposal procedures, staff training, and designated service areas within days, following correct safety standards.

Once official approval was obtained, our motorcycle oil change service acquired credibility and momentum. The excitement of the team soared. They started marking daily goals and pushing themselves to surpass past performance.

"Sir, today we carried out twenty-two oil changes," they would say, with pride. " Tomorrow, let us aim for twenty-25!"

This self-induced rivalry produced a strong culture of success. Team members started researching ways to increase efficiency, cutting service times while preserving quality. From first customer welcome to last documentation, they created systems to handle the flow. The excitement wasn't just about revenue. It was about discovering possibility.

Their creativity and tenacity produced an amazing result, 187 motorcycle oil changes in one day. This was more than just numbers; it was a team's journey from demoralized onlookers in a market crisis to empowered problem-solvers generating their own success.

For a long period, this record was unquestioned and grew to be almost a myth in our network. It was only exceeded when we started teaching the methods created by this innovative team to a passionate group at our Bull Temple Road location, but, as the introduction notes, that is another entirely different story.

We learnt a lot about business resilience from the oil change effort. Looking inwards for nearby prospects using current resources, when outside events make your main business model unworkable.

When dealing with regulations, look for cooperation instead of confrontation. Most importantly, though, when your staff is driven to serve clients, they find innovative ways to channel their enthusiasm, even if clear paths seem closed.

Originally a small idea to keep our team busy during a trying period, it developed into a major service line that not only brought income but also developed customer relationships that would pay off long after fuel price variances normalized.

Sometimes organizations miss growth not because opportunities don't exist, but because nobody pauses long enough to notice patterns

Empowerment is not given—it is designed.

CHAPTER 19

Bull Temple Road Story

"The child who asks questions never becomes lost."

African Proverb

From Saturation to More

Within our network, the Bull Temple Road outlet had developed into something of a myth. Bull Temple Road had its own rhythm—quieter than commercial hubs but deeply rooted in routine customers and neighbourhood familiarity.

Located in the center of Bangalore, this petrol station had accomplished in the lubricant sales area what many would have thought impossible. While most outlets battled to reach even 2 KL per month, this extraordinary team was regularly hitting the 5 KL mark, a figure that had become both their badge of honor and, increasingly, their plateau.

When I visited the outlet for a planned training session, I noticed how it appeared very unlike our usual stations. It looked initially more like a busy automotive workshop than a petrol pump.

Across the forecourt, a long queue of motorcycles and cars with their bonnets opened out. Between vehicles, team members checked oil levels, suggested repairs, and executed the service with trained accuracy. We realized very quickly that copying successful formulas blindly was not going to work here

The operation was remarkable; if you will pardon the pun, a well-oiled machine. Still, the team was not happy to keep the status quo even with their success. Several of the younger team members asked a question that exposed their ambition during a break in our training session.

"Sir, we have been thinking," one of them started, "how do we turn our 5 KL into 8 KL?"

I found their target's specificity to be interesting. The usual 10% or 15% growth targets, which most companies set, were of no interest to them. Their target was a quantum leap, a 60% increase in an operation already running at remarkable rates.

"That's rather a quantum jump," I said. "What makes you think this is even possible?"

Their straightforward but forceful reply was: "Because we believe we haven't reached our full potential yet."

Their appetite for development was contagious. The challenge energized me rather than discounting their aspirational target as unworkable. "Let's have a closer look at your present approach," I advised.

We carefully examined their operation over the next several hours. From first client interaction to last documentation, the team walked me through every stage of their oil change process.

For what it was, the procedure was clearly effective; but a basic limitation became clear: the team had limited capacity to check extra vehicles since so many others were already waiting for service. Their current model had been improved, but within its limitations they had come to a saturation point.

"Here's what I'm seeing," I told the staff following our examination. "Your present model is great for serving your present clientele, but it is not meant to greatly boost volume. While you are missing opportunities with those who come just for fuel, you are serving clients who especially come for oil changes."

The group went through a flash of awareness. They hadn't fully used the much higher flow of clients arriving for regular refueling, having been so preoccupied with fine tuning their oil change service.

"What if you checked quickly for oil right at the fuel islands?" I suggested. "Your staff could check oil levels and suggest changes when necessary while a vehicle is being refilled, which usually takes two to three minutes. For those who agree, you might either schedule them for a convenient time or serve them right away at a designated area."

As the team worked through this concept, their eyes came alive. Without interfering with their current business, this strategy would let them access a far bigger clientele.

"And what about setting aside a lane just for motorcycles?" I carry on. "They take less time for oil changes and refills. For two-wheelers, a separate lane might greatly boost your throughput."

The group jumped at these ideas. They saw chances to break through their ceiling rather than as criticism of their present strategy.

The team leader said, already drawing on a notepad a revised layout for the forecourt, "We'll start implementing these changes immediately."

Impressed by their responsiveness and drive, I left the training session that day unsure whether they would really reach their ambitious target. The 8 KL aim still seemed like a reach.

One month later, I got a picture that stopped me dead-still. Surrounded by empty oil cans set to form the numbers "8.50," the Bull Temple Road team stood boldly on their forecourt, having not only met but surpassed their goal! Their thumbs were raised triumphally, their faces glowing with delight and pride. The breakthrough came only when we stopped trying to impose our model and started understanding the customer's rhythm

By any criteria, what they had achieved was amazing. Within thirty days, they had raised their already outstanding sales volume by sixty percent, surpassing their own ambitious goal. The little adjustments in strategy, adding a dedicated motorcycle lane and checking oil during refueling, had released potential there all along, just waiting to be found.

This success strengthened a principle I have seen repeatedly throughout my career: constraints usually exist mostly in our conception of what's possible, not in the real circumstances we find ourselves in.

To achieve their breakthrough, the Bull Temple Road crew did not require further staff, advanced technology, or even more resources.

They just needed a new viewpoint on their current business practises and the will to apply improvements rapidly and holistically.

Their narrative started to inspire us all across our network. Though few matched the exceptional performance of the original team, other outlets started using their creative approach. Beyond the remarkable figures, I was most struck by how this success had changed the team itself. Their confidence and pride from this success permeated all facets of their business, so fostering a culture of excellence that kept producing outcomes long after this specific milestone.

Business intelligence is often less about data and more about observation

What customers don't know, they can't buy.

CHAPTER 20

Kengeri Story: The "Upanagara" That Scaled Up

"Little by little, one travels far."

Japanese Proverb

Many a time, a keen observation of goings on around training venues provides some of the most insightful analysis of business operations. One such insight came about during a visit to our Shell outlet in Kengeri, a satellite town (Upanagara) outside of Bangalore. The retailer there was also a good friend and former colleague, which especially led to open talks on the difficulties they encountered.

One such discussion about lubricant sales revealed what a young team member thought to be an insurmountable market restriction.

"Sir, you need to understand," he said with the assurance of someone declaring an evident truth, "Since Kengeri is just a satellite town, people here don't have the affordability to buy premium engine oil like synthetic oil."

This comment set off a memory of a similar conversation I had in Thaltej, Ahmedabad, where another "local expert" had explained why his area couldn't get particular results, but that's another tale for another time.

I was intrigued by the young man's certainty about Kengeri's financial restrictions. Instead of right away questioning his presumption, I chose to look for myself.

On purpose, I veered off during our lunch break on a walk to a nearby restaurant. Driven by a basic objective, I started counting luxury cars parked and plying on the streets of this apparently small satellite town. Fascinatingly, I found many Mercedes-Benz, Audi, and BMW models, far more luxury vehicles than budget cars.

This casual observation directly ran counter to the information I had been given on the economic situation of the area. Between perception and reality, something obviously was off. I went back to the outlet after lunch, more conscious now. Nestled in the little, claustrophobic store, I watched a customer searching for engine oil. Not very involved, the cashier just pointed toward the section on oil display.

The sequence that followed was quite instructive. The customer took up a bottle, looked at it momentarily, then put it back on the shelf, he chose a second bottle, quickly put it back, then grabbed a third bottle and almost dropped it in haste. He returned at last to the first bottle and made his purchase.

Fascinated by this choosing process, I subtly investigated the prices of the oils he had under consideration: first ₹197, second ₹374, and third ₹ 525. Under the general belief that "all oils are the same," his behaviour suddenly made perfect sense; he had investigated all possibilities and chosen the most affordable one.

My interest aroused, I trailed the client outdoors to find a mechanic waiting to service his bike. Presumably happy with the transaction, the mechanic quickly changed the oil and sent the customer on his way.

"What do you typically tell consumers about which oil to buy?" I asked the mechanic once the client left.

"Sir, I just tell them to head to the shop, pick up an oil of their choice, and bring it back," he said matter-of-factly.

I turned to look at the wall behind him, where intricate posters showing specific oil recommendations depending on vehicle type and usage pattern hung. "Do you ever guide consumers using those charts?" I questioned.

"No, sir," he said, shrugging slightly. "Those are for consumers to view should they so want."

This little conversation exposed the basic disconnection. The very instruments meant to enable consumers to make wise decisions were considered as only decorations. The professionals, those clients trusted for direction, were totally abdicating their advisory role at the same time.

The next hour, I showed the mechanic how to use the recommendation charts as an active sales tool. We worked on explaining to consumers why a particular oil would be more appropriate for their vehicle and frequency of use. Above all, I underlined the financial aspect of the choice, something that would appeal to consumers with value consciousness.

"Every two months the ₹197 oil needs replacement," I said. "That comes to ₹1,182 a year, with six changes every year. With just three replacements annually, the ₹374 oil needs only three replacements total, actually, less expensive over time. And the premium ₹ 525 synthetic oil is the most cost-effective choice over time since it requires just one annual change.

Processing this data, the mechanic's eyes grew wide. "I never considered it that way," he said. "I thought consumers wouldn't want to pay more upfront, even if it would save money down road."

This little change in strategy, from passive service provider to active advisor, started a remarkable metamorphosis. Previously selling perhaps one premium oil bottle every month, the outlet started selling two or three each shift. The "upanagara" who claimed not to be able to afford luxury goods was suddenly on quite another path.

Who changed? Not the consumers, not the goods, not even the pricing. The team's eagerness to help consumers toward informed decisions instead of letting them negotiate difficult decisions alone set the sole difference.

This encounter strengthened a strong business truth: presumptions about market constraints usually mirror seller attitudes more than real consumer constraints. Kengeri residents were choosing less expensive options since no one had explained why premium options provided better value; they were not avoiding premium oil since they couldn't afford it.

The lesson covers much ground beyond sales of engine oil. Every company looks to us as subject matter experts. They use our direction to negotiate difficult choices. Whether from misguided presumptions about what consumers want or basic resistance to participate, we do a disservice and limit our own business potential when we abdicate this advisory role.

The most successful companies assist their clients in making decisions that really benefit them, not only in terms of products. When done with integrity, this strategy produces the rarest of business results: circumstances whereby everyone really wins.

Though the initial outlay is more, consumers get better value. Companies market products with higher margin. Employees also find great gratification in offering real knowledge instead of only transactional skills.

Potential often hides in places the market has not yet learned to respect.

Constraints don't stop growth—inaction does.

CHAPTER 21

The Thaltej Story

"However beautiful the strategy, you should occasionally look at the results."

Winston Churchill

Examining what people accept as "common knowledge" often reveals powerful commercial insights. That was certainly the case during my visit to our Shell station in Thaltej, a fast-growing suburb of Ahmedabad. The area had a personality of its own—aspirational, fast-changing, and quietly competitive.

The station's performance raised concerns, especially its petrol (Motor Spirit or MS) sales, which consistently trailed network averages. Diesel volumes were steady, but petrol sales stood out as a clear anomaly. We realized quickly that success templates from other locations could not simply be copy-pasted here.

When I asked the team why, one senior attendant replied with confidence, "Sir, it's simple. This area has very few petrol cars." Several others nodded. This wasn't a casual opinion—it was a shared belief. Whenever I hear such certainty around something that doesn't quite add up, I prefer to test it.

During lunch, instead of heading straight to the restaurant, I stood by the main road with a notepad and began counting passing vehicles. Within a short time, I had counted over 200 petrol cars in this supposedly "petrol vehicle scarce" area.

When I shared this with the team, they still pushed back.

"Sir, sab log apne kaam ke vaaste aaye honge," one of them said—suggesting these were not local residents, just people passing through for work.

Fair point. But incomplete.

"Wouldn't they still need fuel?" I asked. "Does it matter whether they live here or not?"

That's when it clicked.

If hundreds of petrol vehicles were moving through the area every day, the issue wasn't demand—it was awareness.

So, we shifted the focus.

"Let's run a local awareness campaign," I suggested. "Let people know we have premium petrol available right here."

What followed was a burst of energy.

The team began discussing ideas—signage at key junctions, outreach to nearby offices, presence during peak hours. What had earlier been dismissed as impossible now felt actionable.

And the results followed.

Petrol sales began to rise within weeks.
Within a month, they had improved significantly.
By the third month, the station was performing above the network average.

Nothing about the market had changed. Only the mindset had.

This experience reinforced a simple but powerful truth:

What we assume to be market limitations are often just operational blind spots.

The team had accepted a story that explained poor performance—and stopped questioning it. Once that assumption was challenged, effort followed. And with effort came results.

Scale rewards standardization. Growth rewards adaptation.

Sometimes, the fastest way to find growth is not to look outward—but to question what we've already accepted as "fact."

CHAPTER 22

The Maninagar Story

"The customer rarely buys what the business thinks it sells."

Peter Drucker

Our work in Ahmedabad came with an ambitious goal.

As part of our Smile–Eye Contact–Tone (SET) training—which later became part of a global template—we aimed to increase premium fuel sales from 2% to 25%. It looked like a steep climb.

Since we were unfamiliar with the local market, we arrived 90 minutes early—not just to be punctual, but to observe.

The first interaction told us a lot.

An auto-rickshaw driver walked in with an empty plastic bottle, asking for petrol. When the staff refused (as per safety norms), he reacted with visible frustration and left in anger.

I had seen this before—in Chennai.

Back then, we had solved it by sending a staff member with a proper container, giving the driver just enough fuel to reach the pump and refill safely.

We tried the same approach here.

It worked.

That moment was reassuring—contexts change, but human responses don't do as much as we think.

As we continued observing, another pattern stood out.

Customers approached with a folded ₹100 note, got exactly ₹100 worth of fuel, and left. No conversation. No suggestion. No engagement.

The staff had built a belief around this. "Customers don't want to talk. If we try, they get irritated." So the system had become simple: take money, dispense fuel, move on.

No wonder premium sales were stuck at 2%.

No tell, no sell.

But then we noticed something interesting.

Some customers held two ₹100 notes. Occasionally, even three.

Clearly, not everyone was locked into ₹100. This wasn't the kind of market where branding alone could win people over. Relationships mattered.

Curious, I asked one such customer,
"If you needed ₹500 worth of fuel, what would you do?"

He smiled and replied,
"Who knows if I'll be alive tomorrow? This is enough for today."

That could have ended the discussion.

Customers had fixed spending limits. Case closed. In places like Maninagar, people don't just evaluate your product. They evaluate your intent

But instead of trying to change behaviour, we reframed the problem:

If customers won't spend more, how can we help them spend better?

The team pointed out a key perception.

Customers believed premium petrol would give them significantly less fuel for the same ₹100—"almost half a bottle less."

So, we tested it. We measured the actual difference.

It turned out to be negligible—barely a water bottle lidful.

That insight changed everything.

The team created a simple visual display using two transparent bottles—one labelled regular petrol, the other premium.

Now, customers didn't need convincing. They could see the difference for themselves. The shift was immediate.

Customers continued spending the same amount—but began choosing premium.

By the end of the day, premium fuel penetration had risen to 42%, far beyond our original target.

What made this work wasn't persuasion.

It was clarity.

We didn't ask customers to spend more.

We helped them make a better choice within what they were already willing to spend.

This experience reinforced an important principle:

Constraints are not always barriers; they can be design inputs.

The team was right about one thing—customers didn't want to spend more. But that insight became useful only when we stopped treating it as a limitation and started working within it.

We knew we were finally being accepted when customers stopped behaving formally with us."

Trust grows slowly, but once earned, it becomes the strongest business asset

Sometimes, growth doesn't come from changing customer behaviour.

It comes from understanding it better.

CHAPTER 23

The Surat Chowdhary Chai Story

"Simplicity executed consistently becomes excellence."

Unknown

Our journey to Gujarat began with a long train ride—from Chennai through Tamil Nadu, Andhra Pradesh, and Maharashtra, before finally reaching Gujarat.

What we expected to be travel turned into a lesson in selling.

Before we left, we were given repeated warnings:

"Gujaratis are extremely price conscious."
"They don't spend unnecessarily."
"What works elsewhere won't work there."

It set the tone.

To distract ourselves, we settled into our books. But what unfolded around us proved far more instructive.

In Tamil Nadu, a chai vendor walked through the compartment calling softly, "Chai, chai."

He barely made eye contact. His energy was low. Passengers had to call him back.

Result: 2 cups sold.

In Andhra Pradesh, the next vendor was slightly better.

"Garma garam chai," he called, making eye contact and pausing occasionally.

Result: 4 cups sold.

In Maharashtra, the pitch evolved further.

"Garam masala chai."

Now there was differentiation. The vendor engaged, paused, and highlighted the product.

Result: 8 cups sold.

Prices moved up too—₹10 in Tamil Nadu, ₹12 in Andhra and Maharashtra.

The link between engagement, positioning, and sales was becoming clear.

But Surat changed everything.

At Surat station, around 4 PM, a team of chai vendors boarded from both ends of the compartment.

They were organised. Confident. Coordinated.

And their pitch was unlike anything we had heard:

"Badhiya wala Chaudhury chai piyo, pasand nahi aaye toh paisa mat do." (Drink the best Chaudhury chai—if you don't like it, don't pay.)

That one line did three things instantly:

- Created curiosity
- Built trust
- Removed risk

Their execution matched their pitch. They worked in pairs—one pouring, one serving and collecting. There was no corporate sophistication here—only rhythm, speed, memory, and human connection. Three such teams covered a single coach with precision.

The result?

In the few minutes the train stopped there, they sold over 60 cups in our coach alone. Passengers—including us—ordered second cups without hesitation.

And the price? ₹15 per cup. Higher than every previous vendor.

This wasn't a price-sensitive market. It was a value-sensitive one.

The vendors had done everything right:

- Clear positioning ("Chaudhury chai")
- Strong value proposition (money-back guarantee)
- Confident delivery
- Efficient execution

And they charged a premium without apology.

This one moment dismantled everything we had been told about the Gujarat market.

When we began training our petrol station teams, we used this example repeatedly.

"Remember the Surat chai vendors," we told them.

"They didn't reduce price. They increased confidence."

As our teams applied this thinking, premium fuel sales began to rise steadily across our network.

That train journey taught us something simple, but powerful:

Markets don't resist price. They resist poor value.

And sometimes, the best lessons don't come from research or reports.

Some businesses grow not because they scale aggressively, but because they become part of people's daily lives."

They come from paying attention to what's happening right in front of you.

CHAPTER 24

The "Late" Arrival of Vishy

"Small daily improvements are the key to staggering long-term results."

Robin Sharma

Back to Qwiky's Coffee Pub—where many of my most valuable lessons came from the most ordinary moments. This one began with Vishy.

He had recently joined us as a part-time employee. It didn't take long to notice he came from an affluent industrialist family—designer clothes, casual references to foreign travel, the occasional appearance of a luxury car. But what stood out wasn't his background. It was his detachment.

Most of our team worked with purpose—either to build a career or support themselves. Vishy treated the job like an optional experience. Something to do, not something to own.

And it showed most clearly in one area: punctuality.

At Qwiky's, we followed a strict "15 minutes early" rule. It gave the team time to prepare, align, and settle into the shift. Everyone followed it. Except Vishy.

He walked in when he pleased—sometimes just on time, often late. Over time, irritation quietly began replacing patience. After a few reminders with no change, I decided to act.

One morning, he walked in late again. I stopped him at the entrance. "Vishy, you know the rule. You'll have to go back home today." He looked stunned. "But I'm just five minutes late."

"That makes it twenty minutes by our standards," I said. "The rule applies to everyone." He paused, unsure how to respond. Then he turned and left—clearly shaken. For him, this wasn't about time. It was about being held accountable. I thought the matter was closed. It wasn't.

Thirty minutes later, the team informed me that a Mercedes had pulled up outside. Vishy stepped out. Behind him, an older man—well-dressed, composed. His father. I knew how this usually goes. A conversation about influence. About flexibility. About "understanding the situation."

I wasn't interested. I stepped out anyway, preparing to defend the decision. Before I could say a word, his father walked up to me and hugged me. Not what I expected. He held my shoulders and said: "Thank you. You taught my son something today that I couldn't." I stood there, silent.

"I wanted him to work so he could understand discipline," he continued. "But he has never been held accountable—not at home, not in college." "Today, for the first time, he experienced what it means to be treated like everyone else." That moment stayed with me. We often assume privilege comes with entitlement. Sometimes, it comes with a gap. A gap that only real-world accountability can fill.

The next day, Vishy arrived twenty minutes early. And he kept doing that. But more importantly, something else changed. He became involved. He started learning, engaging, taking ownership. What had been a casual stint became something meaningful.

Years later, I saw him again—at an airport. He walked up, smiled, and asked, "Do you remember me?" Of course I did. He had gone on to join his family business—but chose to start at the ground level, working his way up. Before we parted, he said something I've never forgotten:

"That day you sent me home—it was the first time anyone held me accountable, regardless of who I was. It changed how I see myself." That incident taught me a few things.

We often underestimate the impact of enforcing standards. We misjudge people based on what we see on the surface. And sometimes, the most valuable thing we can offer someone is not leniency—but fairness.

Leadership becomes dangerous when assumptions replace conversations

Because real privilege is not being excused from standards, it is being shaped by them.

CHAPTER 25

The Venkateshwari Story

"She stood in the storm, and when the wind did not blow her away, she adjusted her sails."

Elizabeth Edwards

When building teams, the most exceptional people don't always come from the most obvious places. That was certainly true when we were hiring for a new Shell outlet.

As part of our search, we visited a training program run by Dr. Reddy's Laboratories as part of their CSR initiative for families affected by the tsunami. We were looking for potential candidates.

We walked into a classroom of about sixty-five trainees. Most were tense, watchful, trying to make an impression. One person stood out.

In a corner sat a young woman—calm, composed, and smiling. While others hesitated, she participated. She asked questions. She listened. There was quiet confidence in the way she carried herself. Without saying it aloud, we all reached the same conclusion. She belonged on our team. Her name was Venkateshwari. That instinct turned out to be right. From her very first day, she showed up with consistency that was hard to ignore. There was a quiet dignity about her that made people instinctively respect her.

Her shift began at 6:00 AM. She reported at 5:30 AM—every single day. Given Chennai's limited early-morning public transport, that wasn't easy. But she never mentioned it. Never used it as an excuse.

Over time, we learnt more about her life. She had two young children. She was in an abusive marriage. Her husband struggled with alcoholism. This job wasn't just employment. It was a lifeline. And yet, none of that showed up in her work. What showed up was energy. Warmth. Presence. Consistency. Life had clearly tested her in ways most people around her would never fully understand. Yet she carried herself not with bitterness, but with remarkable steadiness

In a role where service can easily become mechanical, she remained fully engaged. Customers noticed. One auto driver adjusted his work schedule to match her shift. "I don't start my day unless she is here," he once told me. "Her smile makes the day better." He wasn't the only one. Customers began choosing her island—even when others were free. What she built wasn't service. It was connection.

Her growth within the organisation followed naturally. She didn't chase promotions. She earned them. She became a supervisor—not because of tenure, but because of the way she influenced those around her. She had that rare quality: she lifted the standard of the team without needing to enforce it. A few years later, she got an opportunity to move on—to a managerial role at a Godrej furniture store.

We were proud, and a little reluctant to let her go. But that's when you know you've done your job right. When people outgrow the role, you hired them for.

Venkateshwari's story stayed with me. Not because it was dramatic. But because it was consistent. No formal advantages. No exceptional qualifications. No ideal circumstances. And yet—consistent excellence.

In today's hiring systems, driven by resumes, filters, and keywords, someone like her could easily be overlooked.

On paper, she may not have stood out. In reality, she was exceptional. Her story is a reminder:

Skill can be trained.
Experience can be built.
But character shows up early.

And when someone brings that level of commitment despite difficult circumstances, they don't just grow themselves. They raise the standard for everyone around them.

Some employees contribute more than labour. They contribute perspective."

Excellence is not an event—it is a habit, practised quietly every day.

CHAPTER 26

The Diesel Extra Story

""People believe what they see consistently,
not what they hear occasionally."

Unknown

We had settled into a steady rhythm. Our Shell station ran on very low diesel sales—about 750 litres a day—driven by share autos and a limited window of commercial vehicles due to traffic restrictions. Growth felt capped. Every attempt to scale hit the same wall: customers wanted credit. We were a cash business.

Then came a disruption. Our Territory Manager announced a new product—Diesel Extra, priced ₹1 higher per litre, positioned as a mileage booster. "And how much more volume will you sell with this?" he asked. The question felt disconnected from reality.

We were struggling to grow at existing prices. A premium? With price-sensitive customers? "This will kill our sales," I said. "Our customers won't pay extra." He didn't agree. "You'll do 12,500 litres a day." That was nearly 17 times our volume.

We dismissed it.

On launch day, we prepared to prove him wrong.

We warned every customer about the higher price—and actively turned them away. By noon, we had achieved our goal: Zero sales.

Then something changed. A Tata 407 stopped. The driver insisted on filling ₹300 worth—despite our warnings. He was running a mileage test. Reluctantly, we filled in the Diesel Extra. An hour later, he called back. The results were positive. A larger truck was on its way.

That truck took nearly one hour to fill - 1,500 litres. And while it stood there, something else happened. Other operators noticed. More trucks arrived. Word spread.

By the end of the day: 14,000 litres sold. From 750 to 14,000—in a single day. We had been wrong. Not about price sensitivity—but about value perception.

The premium didn't repel customers. It signalled quality. Fleet operators weren't looking for the cheapest fuel. They were looking for better performance.

Once we shifted from warning about price to explaining value, everything changed. Even our regular customers returned—this time, curious.

The lesson was clear: Customers don't resist higher prices.
They resist unclear value.

CHAPTER 27

The Day We Poured More Into a Pulsar

"A complaint is a chance to turn a customer into a lifelong customer."

Richard Branson

What seemed like a regular day at Shell Vadapalani turned out to be one of the most valuable lessons we learnt in customer service, problem-solving, and exceeding customer expectations. The deepest business learning isn't always the product of a boardroom discussion; they come from on-field challenges that test our resolve to deliver better for the customer.

It was a punishingly hot morning in Chennai. A young man drove in to our forecourt astride his chrome-splashed Bajaj Pulsar 180cc motorcycle. The nature of the request was routine - a simple "full tank, please" - but what followed would shake our understanding of fuel tanks, salesmanship and the measures to which we'll go to win trust.

Our attendant topped up the tank, and when he did the digital readout gave a figure that made us both do a double take: 23.02 litres. The customer's expression visibly changed from nonchalant approval to profound skepticism.

"This can't be happening," he said, the mix of confusion and anger in his voice intensifying. "My bike will never be able to hold that amount of petrol. "You're cheating me."

I knew exactly how his reaction felt. If you are used to paying for 15–18 litres at a time and you see a charge to over 23 litres, that's going to make a pretty big hole in your pocket. In his eyes, we had either made a serious error or were overcharging him.

We immediately offered all standard checks. We showed the calibration certificates for our dispensing devices, explained our quality control measures, and expressed our willingness to have a third party audit our systems. But it wasn't enough to silence his deepening conviction that something was seriously amiss.

This was escalating, and I could tell the conventional wisdom wasn't going to cut it with this customer. His confidence in us was vanishing by the second, and unless we could think of a way out he would leave angry with a story to tell (and a customer lost for good).

That's when I tried a different approach.

"Look," I said, "I know you're really concerned about this. Where are headed today?

"Madurai," he said, still clearly upset. "It's about 500 kilometres away from here."

I had an idea. Why don't you test it out on your ride ? Drive to Madurai if your bike performs and report back. If there's a real problem, we'll fix it."

He looked surprised at me. That wasn't the reply he was expecting from a petrol station manager. Many businesses would have attempted to brush aside his complaint or offer a small payment by way of appeasement. I was rather proposing that his complaint be turned into an experiment.

"You want me to try this for real?" he replied, his indignation giving away to curiosity.

"Absolutely. We believe in our systems, but most importantly we want you to believe as well. There is no better measure of fuel quality and quantity than the performance in the field.

He accepted, but he still looked skeptical. As he rode off, I felt we had just taken a risk, we had either gifted ourselves a devoted customer or the most public sort of problem we didn't yet understand.

We didn't like the uncertainty. We began researching on the 180cc Pulsar's fuel system in right earnest. We looked through tech manuals, automobile forums and manufacturer specs, trying to understand how a motorcycle built for 15-18 litres could take over 23 litres.

We found something interesting about fuel tanks and how capacity is rated. The same goes for the fuel capacity: Converters tend to provide conservative capacity numbers based on usable fuel, not the actual maximum amount that can be stuffed inside the tank. The shape of the tank, the position of the fuel line, venting systems and even the ambient temperature can influence how much petroleum a tank truly holds.

To confirm our findings, we called up our IT support guy, who had a Pulsar 180cc the same model, as ours. In a controlled test, we removed all gas from his tank and filled his tank at our Station. The result was even more startling: 25.7 litres. Rather than ease our concerns, this raised more questions.

The customer returned a week later from Madurai, and he was a completely changed person. The hostility and mistrust had turned to a mix of wonder and gratitude.

"I apologize to you," he began. "The trip was surprising. Typically, I need to fuel up around three-fourths of the way to Madurai, then again at the halfway point on my way back. This time around, my bike made it all the way back to the halfway point on the return leg to Chennai without a fuel halt."

Real-world testing provided proof which even the best tech explanation could not have conveyed. It turned out, that his bike had in fact got the entire fuel we had charged him for, and it had run well.

But the thing that stood out to me the most in this conversation was not the technical vindication but rather the customer's response to our approach. He had never, not once, in the entire course of the episode, raised his voice, spoken in abusive and threatening language, or announced he would be taking his business elsewhere. Why? For the simple reason that from the moment we truly listened to his concern and offered a solution, he felt heard and valued.

"This is something that I could never have dreamt of," he said to us. "Most places would have argued with me or sort of brushed me off. You reassured me and helped me to find out the truth."

We learnt an important lesson about customer service and building relationships. If a customer is worried, it's not simply because they are looking for a fight to pick, or in a dismissive sense, that they're too needy.

They're looking for someone to lock arms with to help them overcome a challenge. Our willingness to spend time and effort addressing his doubt, risky as the venture seemed, had turned a potential complaint into a demonstration of trust and loyalty.

We had later written to Bajaj on this disparity, and we never got a reply. We also found US automotive websites that state based on venting systems and pipeline quantities, fuel tanks can carry 10% more than their declared quantity numbers would suggest. When our customer came back in for his next tank-full, it was to the value of 21 litres which tallied with his view, as he had about 2 litres left after his last fill.

The whole ordeal only served to highlight a core value: when you build relationships of trust and sincere desire to make the customer happy, people will stand beside you rather than against you.

Challenges are opportunities to show what you stand for and how committed you are.

CHAPTER 28

Air Gauge Modification Story

"Leadership is not about being in charge.
It is about taking care of those in your charge."

Simon Sinek

Innovation rarely comes from boardrooms. More often, it comes from people doing repetitive work long enough to become frustrated by it.

Our fuel station had a unique problem—one most businesses would have happily accepted.

Customers loved our free air service. A little too much.

On an average day, we served nearly 7,800 fuel customers. But the number of air requests crossed 10,000 daily. Many customers came only for air. Two-wheelers, cars, autos, delivery vehicles, vans—there was a constant stream of vehicles lined up near the air bays from morning till night.

At first, we were proud of it.

Good service creates traffic. Traffic creates reputation.

But slowly, another reality started emerging.

The air stations had become one of the most exhausting places to work in the outlet.

We had four air stations and four attendants dedicated to handling them through full shifts. Unlike fuel attendants, there were no incentives, no commissions, and certainly no tips waiting at the end of the day. Just nonstop repetitive movement.

"Sir... I didn't notice, was busy on phone, can you show pressure once more?"

"Sir... Can you fill the spare tyre as well."

"Sir... looks like I have a puncture, fill it up till I reach a tyre shop."

"Sir... check back tyre again please."

Every vehicle needed a different pressure setting. Every request meant movement. Bend down. Check pressure. Walk back to the machine. Adjust settings. Walk back again. Recheck. Repeat.

Hundreds of times a day.

From a distance, the work looked easy and simple.

From close quarters, it was physically draining. Chennai heat made it worse.

The attendants rarely complained openly, but fatigue had started showing up in other ways—irritation, slower response, reduced enthusiasm, occasional arguments among themselves about shifts and rotation.

One of the biggest mistakes organizations make is assuming repetitive work is easy work.

In reality, repetition creates a different kind of exhaustion.

We had two choices. Reduce the service. Or rethink the system.

Thankfully, the team chose the second option.

The first improvement was surprisingly simple.

Rotation.

Instead of permanently assigning the same employees to the air stations, we began rotating responsibilities across the team. The impact was immediate. Energy levels improved. Complaints reduced. Even the mood at the air stations became lighter.

But the real breakthrough came from the frontline itself.

One afternoon, an attendant casually said:

"Sir… what if we had a remote to control pressure?"

At first, it sounded almost amusing.

Remote control? For an air machine?

But the more we listened, the more sense it made.

The real problem was not the pressure adjustment itself. The real problem was the constant walking back and forth between the customer's vehicle and the machine.

A customer would ask for 32 PSI.

The attendant would walk to the control unit.

Adjust.

Walk back.

Check.

Then the customer would say:

"Sir… little more."

Back again.

For thousands of vehicles.

Every single day.

The breakthrough didn't come from technology.

It came from paying attention.

That is something many organizations miss. Frontline teams usually know exactly where the inefficiencies are. They live inside the process every day. Unfortunately, very few people ask them enough questions.

There was only one problem.

No such product existed.

So, we decided to build one ourselves.

With the help of a local engineer, the team started experimenting with a simple remote-control mechanism that could regulate pressure settings without requiring attendants to walk repeatedly to the machine.

It was not some fancy Silicon Valley innovation.

No glossy presentation.

No innovation workshop.

Just a practical solution born from tired legs and daily frustration.

But once implemented, the impact was dramatic.

Attendants moved less.

Fatigue reduced.

Service speed improved.

Queues moved faster.

Customers experienced quicker turnaround times.

And interestingly, the attendants themselves became more cheerful while handling customers.

Sometimes employee frustration quietly leaks into customer experience without organizations realizing it.

Something as simple as smoother airflow management suddenly changed the customer experience dramatically.

The biggest lesson for me was this:

The people closest to the problem are usually closest to the solution.

Organizations spend enormous amounts of money searching for innovation externally while completely ignoring the intelligence already present within their teams.

Most employees may not speak the language of management consultants or engineers.

But they understand friction.

And people who experience friction daily often understand solutions better than anyone else.

Operational excellence is often invisible to customers—until it is missing.

The best systems are not always the most sophisticated ones.

They are the ones that make life easier:

- For customers
- For employees
- And for the business at the same time.

That little air-pressure remote never made headlines.

But for the people working those shifts every day, it changed everything.

The people closest to the problem are closest to the solution.

CHAPTER 29

The Observation Jockey Story

"Most people look. Very few truly observe."

Unknown

As a person in the hospitality profession, from time to time, you meet people who have a strong sense of curiosity about the world that makes their approach to their work uniquely distinctive.

These are the folks who don't just do their jobs, but who seem to absorb everything around them, like giant sponges of knowledge, always learning, always growing, always wanting to understand more than what's called for in their job descriptions. Venkatesh was one of those extraordinary people and his story is a testament to the power of initiative, curiosity and the courage to look beyond the ordinary.

I first met Venkatesh when I was working for a hotel, and he was part of the housekeeping team. From the start, there was something unusual about the way he worked that intrigued me. Most employees in his position concentrated all their energy on performing their immediate duties—to clean rooms, to keep the premises in good repair, and to follow standard operating procedures—but Venkatesh's curiosity about every aspect of the hotel seemed endless.

He noticed details most people filtered out as background noise. It wasn't just that he was committed to his own primary responsibilities, which he was. It was his natural curiosity about how the different departments worked and how systems were connected, and how guests had an experience throughout the hotel.

He'd show up early and stay late, not because he had to, but because he was truly fascinated by all of the moving parts of running a hotel. What others dismissed as routine behaviour, he treated as useful information

During slack times, when all the other employees scattered to break rooms or went out of their way to pass their time, Venkatesh went into other departments and watched how things worked, asked questions (some of which were thoughtful), and formed relationships with co-workers around the entire organisation. He built relationships with department heads—not by flattering, but by showing genuine interest in their work and a willingness to learn from their expertise.

His mind was methodical and deliberate. He would shadow the front office, delving into how reservation systems worked, how guests checked in, even the balance on maintaining the flow of inventory in a room. He shadowed maintenance workers, learning the mechanical systems and the difficulties that can arise from trying to keep a complex facility functioning. He'd watch how food and beverage operations worked, from menu planning to kitchen logistics to the juggling it took to serve hundreds of meals each day.

What stood out most was this: He was good at connecting the dots across multiple departments that others couldn't. He knew that housekeeping was not only about cleaning rooms, but also about laying the foundation for guest satisfaction that would resonate through every other part of the hotel stay.

He understood how activities in the front of the house affected housekeeping schedules, how things back of the house could adversely affect guests and how important food and beverage could be to a hotel's reputation.

His superiors and peers started to get used to his can-do nature and his impressively expanding learning capacity. But whereas employees walked in thinking their role was to complete a description of work, Venkatesh saw his actions as part of a bigger cause: to create outstanding moments for guests. It was this mindset that truly set him apart, not only on housekeeping, but across operations excellence.

When I moved from hotel industry to Qwiky's Coffee Pub, the first name on my list of recruits was Venkatesh. I'd seen him go from a solid but unremarkable employee to his being a potential superstar, and I knew that the combination of hard work, curiosity, and learning ability were going to be incredibly valuable for us as we got started.

His crossing over to Qwiky's was smooth and surprising. He worked our entry level job, as a courtesy crew cleaning up and helping customers.

But as he had in the hotel, he quickly learnt all aspects of our operations. He discovered how to make coffee, how to treat customers, how to close out inventory, and how retail even functioned far beyond his role as "courtesy crew".

He rose quickly through our ranks and that was well-earned. He worked his way up from courtesy crew to Barista to Shift Manager to Project Manager, running stand-alone projects with the same level of diligence and concern he had shown since day one. Each promotion was earned through display of competence and relentless pursuit of excellence.

But Qwiky's wasn't the end of Venkatesh's tale. This path of lifelong learning and development had not just taught him job skills; it had also given him the confidence and knowledge to act on his own entrepreneurial dreams. He went on to create his own chain of tea shops, using all his training in hospitality, customer service, operations management, and business development.

I was so proud and happy to hear about his business success. Here was a man who had begun as a humble housekeeper and used his curiosity, dedication, and "I-think-I-can- and-I-will" learning model to create his own business empire. His success wasn't the reflection of a proper education, or any inherited privileges; it was a manifestation of an insatiable thirst for knowledge, learning and growing.

Venkatesh's story says something profound about career and life growth. In today's hyper-evolving economy, the most precious employers and entrepreneurs are not always the job candidates who look best on paper or start at the highest rung.

They're the people who approach their work with a sense of genuine curiosity, who recognize learning opportunities in all scenarios, and who grasp that today's entry-level position can be tomorrow's opportunity to soar.

His own path also illustrates the value of mentorship and visibility in career development. Sometimes it is the act of a true-leader—one who can recognize talent in seemingly unlikely places and offer a chance for what lies dormant within to come out into the light. And by acknowledging Venkatesh's great attitude and affording him opportunities to learn and hone his skills, we not only had a wonderful team player on board but have somehow paid forward to his unique transformation.

The bigger takeaway from Venkatesh, he says, is that one's career trajectory is not handcuffed to job titles, educational qualification or starting positions. It's fueled by attitude—by curiosity and the determination to see all experiences as learning opportunities. Whether you are a hotel housekeeping staff or a coffee-shop courtesy crew, there is honestly great potential for growth out there if you badly want it.

His observation skills were exceptional and boy, did he observe a lot? He used to spend extra hours at work just to learn and when it came to implementing, he was indeed a thoroughbred jockey. Observation is not passive. Done properly, it becomes a competitive advantage.

The ones who pay attention are the ones who move ahead.

CHAPTER 30

The Water in the Tank Story

"What is unseen often matters most."

Unknown

It's the time of year when monsoon rains flood the city, inundating streets and putting the city's infrastructure and its businesses to the test. It was in the middle of one of those downpours when we learnt one of the most important lessons about client relationships, crisis communication, and the clear difference between transactional interactions and real partnerships that are rooted in trust and mutual respect.

The rain had been coming down for what seemed like several hours. During that deluge our Shell station never closed, servicing those customers who dared to navigate flooded streets to keep their cars running. We took pride in continuing service during inclement weather, as it was part of our commitment to the community. Everything appeared normal on the surface—which is often the most dangerous stage of a problem.

What we didn't see, when our attention was focused on keeping operations running, was that all the water collecting in the street was making its way into our underground storage tanks. Heavy rain, poor drainage and inevitable imperfections in underground fuel storage combined in a way that would soon put everything we thought we knew about customer service and crisis response to the test.

The night was winding down as usual when my phone rang at about 9 pm. The voice at the other end was that of a customer who had bought diesel from us sometime earlier in the day and had been stranded on the highway that led to Tirupathi with his Tata Sumo, full of family members, on a pilgrimage.

"Sir, there seems to be something wrong with the Diesel I got from your station," he said, calmly. "My car has broken down, and we've discovered water in the diesel tank.

My heart sank. This was a fuel retailer's worst-case scenario—tainted fuel that could lead to vehicle failures, costly repairs and, in the worst case, dangerous scenarios for customers on long trips.

But then something surprising came next. There were no furiously worded complaints, no threats of suing or demands for immediate reimbursement; this customer had a different concern altogether.

"I'm calling to ask you to halt the sale of diesel immediately until they can have the tanks checked," he added. "I'm concerned for other customers who may encounter the same issue, and particularly for those that have to travel long distances.

I was stunned. Here, the customer was stuck in a strange land, facing significant hassles and a potential huge cost of repair, and rather than focus on himself, his first thought was of us and our other customers, to keep them from having the same problem he did. His empathy and civic-mindedness and the concern he felt for his fellow drivers was both rare and profoundly moving.

We promptly followed his advice and stopped selling diesel as we tried to work out the level of contamination. The technical report was confirmation of our worst fears: the prolonged rainfall had infiltrated our underground storage area, and the water had mingled with the diesel.

As the sun rose the next morning, we began to understand the scope of the disaster. Our sources told us that nearly 49 vehicles had taken the bad diesel and had broken down with varying degrees of damage spread all over Chennai and beyond. The customers came to us in a steady stream, each with a story of inconvenience, broken appointments and mechanical failure.

I steeled myself for what I anticipated would be a day of confrontations, blowups and escalation. Customers who find out they have purchased contaminated fuel that wrecked their car usually show up angry, demanding and prepared to fight. The risk that this would explode into a PR disaster and legal implications were massive.

But something remarkable happened instead. How we managed each interaction with a customer dictated how the overall crisis would develop.

From the first customer at the door, we embraced the practise of full transparency, instant accountability, and immediate (positive) action. We did not make excuses, did not seek to minimize the problem and did not resort to the defensive posturing that so often occurs when businesses find themselves in such situations involving legal liability.

"We're truly sorry this took place," I would say to every customer. "We're taking full responsibility to ensure this never happens again, your satisfaction is our highest priority, and we'll make the situation right—at no cost to you—as soon as possible," it said.

We proposed that we would either fix any harm done by the contaminated fuel or pay fair damages for the problem that our customers faced. We didn't need prolonged investigations, the need for numerous estimates, or bureaucratic red tape. All we did was to ask each customer what we could do to make the situation right and then tried to deliver those remedies in a fair and expedited manner.

Our customers' reaction was amazing. Instead of the hostile environment I'd expected, we found ourselves partnering with people who valued our no-nonsense approach and real desire to help them. We could have been haunted by our badly affected customers, but they became our collaborators in seeking just resolutions.

One vivid exchange was a small business, whose delivery van had broken down enroute to an important customer's appointment. Instead of insisting on a punitive sum, he sat down with us to assess the damage and the lost business, and he agreed to our paying for the mechanical repairs and for the business he lost. He went on to say to other customers while we waited in the office that he had "never had a company call him back so fast and deliver so promptly and fairly".

Another customer (a teacher who broke down on the way to a medical appointment for her elderly parents) not only accepted our offer to pay for repair and substitute transport arrangements but also sang our praises to her neighbours and co-workers about our management of the crisis.

By the time what might have been our worst business day was over, we had settled every one of their cases to the customers' satisfaction.

Most importantly, what we gained was priceless: the respect and loyalty of customers who had seen us at our lowest, and who were there when we had unwavering commitment to doing the right thing, no matter the cost or inconvenience.

The loss of revenue, as we were forced to clean up the mess, was significant; it was expensive, we paid for repairs, paid for clean-up, and incurred all the other expenses that come with a crisis of this nature. But the long-term gains were far worth these short-term costs. The customers who experienced our crisis management emerged as some of our biggest fans speaking about how fairly and honestly, we had treated their issues.

This experience taught us that reputation in customer service is not built during easy times when everything goes right. It is made during a crisis, when businesses must decide whether they're going to defend their own interests or defend their customers.

By opting for the customer's best interest over the financial aspect, we ultimately formed ongoing relationships that would extend beyond the event.

Standards are not maintained through inspections alone. They survive through ownership.

Reputation is not built in good times—it is revealed in difficult ones.

CHAPTER 31

The Prakash Story

"People blossom when they feel seen."

Unknown

Sometimes, the biggest transformations don't come from systems or strategies—but from understanding people. During a training session at our Thaltej outlet, the energy in the room was high. Most participants were engaged, asking questions, participating in exercises. Except one.

Prakash sat in the corner. Silent. Withdrawn. Disconnected. It wasn't just his lack of participation that stood out—it was how others treated him. There were jokes, dismissive comments, and clear social exclusion. He wasn't just disengaged; he was isolated.

When I asked about him, the responses were predictable. "He's always like this." "He doesn't want to learn." A label had been assigned. And accepted.

Experience has taught me that behaviour is often a surface signal, not the root issue. So instead of pushing him in the session, I chose a different approach. During the break, I asked him to join me for tea across the street. He hesitated—but agreed.

At the tea stall, something interesting happened. The shop owner greeted Prakash with visible respect—far more than he showed me.

That contrast was telling. There was clearly more to this story. As we spoke, the pieces fell into place. Prakash came from a once-prominent local family. They had owned land in the area—land on which our petrol station now stood. But the family had lost everything. His father, once a landowner, now worked as a watchman. The fall was public. And painful.

That explained everything.

His silence.
His withdrawal.
His discomfort at work.

He wasn't disengaged. He was carrying shame.

I looked at him and asked, "Do you know what your name means?" "Light," he said quietly. I pointed to the sunlight entering the room. "What is this light doing?" He paused, then said, "It brightens the place."

"Exactly," I said. "That's your role—not just here, but in your own life." Something shifted.

Not dramatically. Not instantly. But enough.

Back in the session, he began participating. Tentatively at first. Then with increasing confidence. His local knowledge—once hidden—became valuable. His peers began to see him differently.

And within weeks, he became one of the stronger performers on the team.

Nothing about his circumstances changed. Only his self-perception did.

The lesson is simple:

Behind every disengaged employee is a story.
Find it—and you change the outcome.

CHAPTER 32

The Mahesh Story - Magadi Pulsar Premium Full Tank

"Nothing great was ever achieved without enthusiasm."

Ralph Waldo Emerson

There are some barriers that hold back or stifle the highest potential in individuals. These barriers are not always about knowledge or skills—they often have to do with the way the individual perceives themselves, how confident they are, and the stories people create in their lives when it comes to what they can or cannot do. Mahesh was one such guy, a self-doubting youngster who later became a star sales resource.

Mahesh was a young team member from a difficult background, struggling with confidence rather than capability. He was a short guy with a few physical challenges that held him back from life. His physical challenges were the least of his problems, what held him back was his self-confidence, and the attitude he had grown up believing about how much he was worth and what he was capable of.

His self-talk during our initial training showed his mindset. He would downplay himself and things that happened whenever he was asked about his life.

He sounded like he was denying himself as he spoke, always undermining his own message, damaging his own credibility in the listener's ear before what he was saying had finished coming out of his mouth.

"I don't know if I have it in me," was his common refrain. "People like me don't usually do well at this.". His posture reinforced this - shoulders hunched forward, eyes clearly averted away, voice barely above a whisper whenever he spoke, if at all.

We were in the middle of doing a training program on up-selling, with a clear focus on selling premium fuel. The session was created to assist our team members to map ways to add value to our customers and increase average revenue per transaction. The kind of training that could change a person's career trajectory—if they were willing to apply it with confidence.

The one we happened to be talking about was when a customer brings in a new motorcycle – here is a chance to develop a relationship that could potentially last over ten years. We walked through the entire approach: how to engage with a new vehicle owner, how to start the conversation by congratulating them on their great decision, and how to present premium service and maintenance products as critical care for their new purchase.

"The trick is to think of it as a service for the customer, who will get something no one else can offer, and not as a transaction. A first-time bike owner plans to safeguard their investment and keep it looking new. We're helping them do that."

The training covered the full ecosystem on how a motorcycle can be taken care: premium fuel protecting the engine, high end oils to enhance performance, cleaning products to maintain appearance, helmet care for safety items, chain maintenance to maintain the machines.

Each item had true value for someone who had recently spent a lot of money on a new bike. As we acted out these scenarios, Mahesh's nervousness was evident. As the rest of the team tried out their approaches with great zest, he sat quietly, shaking his head from time to time in disbelief.

"Do you really think I can ask customers these questions?" he inquired during a break; his voice tinged with doubt. "Do you think they would agree to buy these things from someone like me?"

His was the kind of question that rests deep down within many of us. He wasn't doubting the value of the products or the approach itself—he was doubting his worthiness to suggest them.

"Definitely yes," I answered without a doubt. "You get these products, you understand the benefits of them, and you also care about helping the customer protect their investment. That's all you need."

After a long lunch and on our way out to start up the next training module, Mahesh was about to start his fuel island shift. Best of all the timing was excellent – he'd get to use the stuff he learnt right away.

Something interesting happened, about half an hour into his shift. Mahesh ran into our training center, his face lit up with excitement.

"Sir! Sir!" his voice crackling with excitement. "You won't believe what just happened!

To see this sprightly, confident young man here, and remember the timid creature who came to the outlet to prepare for his shift, was most certainly a pleasant surprise. We paused the session and asked him to share his experience. "We found a paint can, and we turned it upside down," I called out to the group. "Mahesh, come up here and tell us your story."

Standing before the group, Mahesh narrated his experience with visible excitement of a person who had stumbled upon a new superpower.

"A guy brought in this brand-new Yamaha superbike," he started, his voice now clear and strong." He requested only ₹50 worth of fuel, but I recalled what we were taught regarding new bike customers.

Mahesh had done just what he had been trained to do. He congratulated the customer on a great choice of vehicle, pointed out how premium fuel would keep the engine clean from the very first day of ownership, and presented the entire care product line as mandatory purchases to ensure investment in bike performance and appearance.

"I said exactly what we had been taught," Mahesh proceeded, encouraged by his own confidence. "I talked to him about premium fuel and keeping his engine clean and about specialized oil that would protect his investment and care products to keep his bike looking showroom fresh." On a busy forecourt, where most conversations last less than a minute, he somehow managed to make customers engage.

Not only did the customer accept filling the whole "whatever" with top-of-the-line gas, but also bought cleaning products, helmet cleaner and chain spray. What's more, he'd been so impressed with Mahesh's intelligence and caring nature that he'd even had a selfie taken with him before he left.

"He spent ₹1,600 on the whole," Mahesh declared with pride. "One guy came in to get ₹50 of fuel and bought ₹950 of premium fuel and ₹650 of care products. And he thanked me for helping him with his new bike"

It was a total turning point. In the moment of a single successful exchange, Mahesh had just found out something life-changing about himself – he had value to deliver to customers, he earned a ton of trust and gratitude, and he was able to produce results, which seemed impossible just a few minutes back.

What was especially powerful about that story was the customer's response. The selfie wasn't just a casual photo—it was an acknowledgment of the value Mahesh had brought. The customer was naturally thankful for the help and advice and had almost made Mahesh his adviser rather than just the petrol station staff.

The momentum from this accomplishment reverberated well past that single purchase. The way Mahesh's self-image transformed, his confidence increased significantly and his attitude to every meeting that followed was totally different. He realized that his history, his size, his experience—all of those things—didn't matter when he was committed to creating real value for real customers.

But, more importantly, Mahesh discovered a key principle of sales success: It's not about manipulation or pressure; it's about knowing what a customer needs and offering a solution that's good for them. The customers' thanks and desire to have a photo taken showed that looking at sales as service pays off for everyone.

This moment was as much of a game changer for Mahesh as it was for our curriculum more generally. It showed how, with the right attitude, training and the guts to make the most of it, results can be significant, no matter where you begin. Customers respond differently when service feels enthusiastic instead of mechanical

Sales is not just about the product—it's about the belief behind it.

CHAPTER 33

The Kid Who Would not Smile

"Too often we underestimate the power of a touch, a smile, a kind word."

Leo Buscaglia

The most successful outcomes are frequently due to small things that rest in customers' hearts. In industries where products are standardised and prices are fixed; customer experience becomes the key differentiator. This is the tale of how we built our trademark customer service style and how a veritable naysayer of a team member's conversion led to a training method that would touch thousands throughout the network.

We were at the Varthur site of Shell (again) and pitching (one of the bids that) has been the game changer for us as small fledgling entrepreneurs in training. Two bigger, more experienced rivals had already made their pitches, wowing our former colleagues with slick pitches from a proven business. We had been the underdogs, armed with only passion, fresh ideas—and lacking the credentials to ordinarily win such contracts.

It was the very definition of a deceptively simple, though epically difficult, ask to instill confidence in front-line workers. We knew, and we still know, that confidence was/is the basis of great customer service.

Confident staff members will smile easily and discuss with confidence, they will make good eye contact, and they'll make positive customer service engagements that remain long after the sale is over.

As we made our way towards the venue, chatting about our work, the answer to our language barrier problems suddenly came to me in the unlikeliest of places: a snippet of conversation that I overheard in the local language while crossing a busy street. Then someone said "set agiddiya maga", and the word "SET" just hit us. It was perfect – a simple, universally recognized word which transcended all Indian languages and expressed the exact sentiment we wanted to convey.

But what did it mean to be "SET"? We discussed the actions confident people naturally take. They smile and form emotional bonds with others. They speak knowledge and assurance in a confident tone. They look into your eyes, indicating presence and attention. We called it SET: -Smile, Eye Contact and Tone – a simple yet powerful acronym that helped tens of thousands of customer service attendants manifest confidence.

The acronym was beautiful in its simplicity," but we also realized that true change would be in the carrying out, not just the idea. We were excited to explain our approach, and thankfully our excitement translated into some momentum. We won the training contract, and it was the start of an incredible journey for both- us as trainers and for the hundreds of staff we gradually trained.

The rubber met the road when we started to apply SET in real operations. Our team was quick to adopt the framework, and most members felt comfortable with it almost immediately. This allowed them to witness immediate impacts on their customer interactions, and they also experienced the positive vibes that emanated from the nature of more engaging service delivery.

Yet one of the team members was a tough nut to crack and a real test for our entire approach. There was something unusually withdrawn about him, especially compared to the noise and excitement around him.

He was a part-time student at a college, and his father was also employed at the same station. It was a source of profound resentment, rather than motivation. The young man resented his father for what he considered the situation in his family, and this resulted in a refusal to comply with the work in a good way.

Whatever we did—asking, encouraging, explaining why good customer service is important—he wouldn't budge. His smile was what was missing, it just didn't seem right for us to meet the SET protocol without it. It really came to a head when we decided for him to perform a field exercise that would have shown Shell's management we were training him effectively.

"This is one of the most important moments in your life," I said to him, in an attempt to get through to him. "Other than the day of your wedding, this moment could be the most important in terms of your career. "Can you at least smile when it counts for this test, please?"

Something about saying his future wedding made him feel this message more intensely. His face softened for an instant, and he nodded and smiled cheerfully. We took a quick photo of it and showed it to him.

"Look," we said, showing him the picture. ‚This is what smile looks like on you. This is the face customers want to be greeted with."

The images of the evidence seemed to speak to him in ways our words had not. He stared at the photo, as if seeing himself anew. "I'll smile when it makes the most sense," he said quietly.

It just so happens the evaluation was the ideal litmus test for his stamina. At our station, a Jonga, a utility vehicle, pulled up asking for a full tank of diesel. Our somewhat unwilling team member instead sidled up to the car and produced the finest example of the SET framework I had ever seen.

So sincere was the smile, so cheerful the tone, so professional the attitude, so correct the style of eye contact. The interaction with the customer was perfect - it was **exactly** what we were training our entire staff on and trying to get them to do.

But then something magical occurred. The passenger door of the Jonga flew open, and a stylishly attired lady alighted. She went straight over to one of our staff members and broke into a huge smile.

“Young man,” she said, “I have to shoot your picture.

Then she whipped out a Polaroid camera and snapped him in the now, grinning from ear to ear, looking completely natural and uncoerced. And she handed him the photo developed a minute prior and told him why this moment meant so much to her.

“I’ve been going around the world for 35 years,” she said, with a voice that carried warmth. “I’ve collected photos of my travels and photographed at thousands of petrol stations in various countries. But you know what? Not once have I seen a smiling petrol pump attendant until now.

She went so far as to do the most unimaginable thing. She signed the picture, cementing the moment of triumph forever.

The change was immediate and sustained. This young man, who for months had rejected all attempts to instill customer engagement skills in him had just been set a personal example of how customer service is done. A man he had never seen before, a world traveler with decades of life experience was able to see something special in his labour and she made time to acknowledge it in person.

The Polaroid, rather than simply a keepsake, seemed to represent possibility and change. For the first time in his working life, this unhappy employee had tasted the real joy that comes of giving another human being a bright spot in his or her day.

This one exchange had a ripple effect that went far beyond. His relationship with work, his relationship to customers and his relationship to his own potential changed dramatically.

That hitherto hard-pressed smile came easy and often. He gained confidence, did better in his job and, most significant, learnt that he could find meaning in his work by making other people happy.

This became a central story in our training programs showing that anyone could deliver outstanding service when they realize what is at stake. That photo and story went through our network, and so many others on our team that had confidence or motivation issues were moved by it.

It was its realness that made here so inspiring. It wasn't a staged performance or a scripted exchange—it was a real moment between two people, something that yielded mutual pleasure and recognition. Our team members' pride was well-deserved, and the customer's gratitude was genuine.

A smile is not a skill you're taught—it's a value you choose. People don't remember the service—they remember how you made them feel.

CHAPTER 34

The "Sell Me a Pen" Story

"Whether we realize it or not, all of us are selling something every day—ideas, trust, confidence, or ourselves."

Unknown

Sometimes life has a somewhat funny way of teaching us something repeatedly until a lesson gets in! At other times the lessons arrive disguised as problems we think we can avoid, opportunities we think we do not need, or truths we are not yet prepared to face. This is the story of how a basic pen became the emblem of my sharpest professional education and, ultimately, informed my definition of what it means to really sell, influence and connect with people.

The introduction to the seemingly simple problem came at a regular campus recruitment interview with Sterling Resorts. It was the era of the Gulf War, at a time when scarce, precious job opportunities seemed like a mirage. 23 of my batchmates had already got placed while on campus, and I had explicit advice against appearing for any more interviews given that I was already placed with Hindustan Motors.

But human nature—and, in the case of recent grads, that natural competitive instinct—made me wonder what I was missing. When I learnt about the opening in Sterling Resorts for a job, I became curious to see what the role was all about.

The room used for interviews was intimidating, an imposing room – big, formal, a room that was designed to intimidate candidates. The interviewer—already a hand with many years of experience at hiring and interviews—had obviously gone through thousands of interviews. Sitting across from him, proud of my academic accomplishments and general aptitude, I had no idea that I was about to be asked a question that would shed light on the very gap in my knowledge of professional life.

"Take this," he said, passing me a plain ballpoint pen. "Sell this pen to me."

It was a ridiculous, and even offensive, request. And here I was, a fresh yet-to-be graduate with passable smarts, asked to do what looked like a dumb assignment. It was an immediate, and in hindsight, embarrassingly pompous response.

I pushed the pen across the table with some disdain. If I ever must sell anything I'd rather die," I announced, irony completely lost on me, moments after having applied for a job in sales.

The interviewer let me walk toward the door with my pride unfazed and ignorance intact. But as I reached for the handle, he pulled me back.

"Young man," he said, and there was laughter and wisdom in his voice, "it's better to die, there's not a moment in life when you will not sell something or the other.

I stared at him with what can only be pity. I was young, I was a cocky git, I felt that he was the one who didn't understand.

I resolved to track him down 10 years later and demonstrate the degree to which selling was not actually needed in life. I was going to prove to him you could be successful in life and never have to "sell" anything.

Now, decades later, I earn a living teaching individuals how to sell. The irony is not lost on me. The man I once pitied for having a narrow worldview got a principle of human exchange that I for years did not: that a person does not treat others according to who they are but instead treats others according to who he is.

The second time I met the pen-selling challenge was in a separate phase of my career, when I was doing an executive training program at a hotel. Unbeknownst to my trainer who didn't know my history with this lesson, passed stuff around for participants to use in a sales simulation.

Or fate had a sense of humor, as they say. And what did I get—a pen, of course.

"I can't sell a pen," I protested to the trainer right away. "Give me something else."

His answer questioned yet another assumption which I had been wearing for years. "You don't always get to pick and choose in life," he said, calmly. "You can't always get what you want."

The man could teach a thing or two about more than just how to sell things—he could show them about how to adapt, about resourcefulness, about finding value in what life throws in the way. But I wasn't yet prepared to hear that message.

"I have no knowledge on this pen or product," I said, dredging for explanations. "I have to know what I'm selling before I sell."

What came next would be a turning point in how I thought about sales, persuasion, and the power of storytelling.

That pen," the instructor replied, as cool as Cool cucumber, "Well that was the pen Winston Churchill used to sign the World War treaty.

Suddenly, everything changed. With a pen that was once just another ballpoint, in my outstretched hand, I held history: a weapon that influenced global affairs, a relic that told a story outside of its use.

With that one sentence I sold the pen for a lakh of rupees (of course, it was only a notional transaction, and no money ever actually changed hands). The other members of the room were not swayed by the pen's functionality, but by its story, its past, and the emotional connection that story sparked.

This episode spoke volumes about the meaning of selling – indeed, about human nature itself. People don't purchase products—they buy stories, they buy experiences, they buy solutions to problems, they buy emotional connections. There had been no material change in the physical characteristics of the pen, only a radical change in the perceived value of it through the power of the story.

It was that Sterling Resorts interviewer, trying to teach me something years ago, coming to visit me all over again. Selling is more than retailing in a store.

Every day, we sell our ideas to coworkers, our vision to employees, our capacity to employers, our point of view to friends and family. We sell our children on the value of education, our spouses on where we should vacation, ourselves on why we should take certain risks and chase opportunities.

Leadership is selling, plain and simple, convincing others to believe in (read: vote for, contribute to, buy) your vision. Parenting is selling—convincing children to make good choices. And marriage, it's selling—always be selling your value as a partner. Career progress is selling—selling yourself to bosses and to companies.

The pen exercise showed me that objections are often the result of more meaningful problems. My reaction wasn't really about the pen at all—it was about my unease with influence, my misunderstanding of sales, and my inability to comprehend how value is generated and conveyed.

Today, when I meet fresh graduates who feel they are too good to be sales reps, or too good to have to learn to sell, I share the story with them. Not because I'm trying to get them to be salespeople – but because I think that influence and persuasion and value creation are life skills that go far beyond job titles or industry verticals.

The pen I refused to sell had come to symbolize a critical career lesson for me. It showed me how every time we speak is an opportunity to add value, that storytelling is the most forceful technology of humanity and that the ability to connect, to influence, to persuade can shape our lives in personal and professional ways.

The exercise was never really about the pen. It was about understanding need before offering solution

When you add meaning, you create value.
And when value is clear, selling becomes natural.

CHAPTER 35

The Cartoon War Against Food Wastage at Hindustan Motors

"Sometimes the smallest step in the right direction
ends up being the biggest step of your life."

Unknown

I walked into my first job at Hindustan Motors on June 1, 1993—fresh out of college, full of intent, and quietly determined to make a difference.

Like most new entrants, I started by observing. Understanding how things worked, who mattered, and where I could contribute meaningfully.

That's when I noticed something unsettling.

The cafeteria, which fed hundreds of employees every day, was generating nearly **1,500 kilos of food waste daily**. Not because the food was bad or inedible—but because people were simply taking more than they could eat. Like in many cafeterias, people had become so used to seeing food wasted that it barely registered anymore.

Plates were piled high. Meals barely touched. And then discarded. This wasn't an occasional issue. It was routine. Accepted. Almost invisible. The more I watched, the more it bothered me.

This wasn't just food being wasted. It was effort. Cost. Energy. Intent. And somewhere, there is a complete disconnect between consumption and consequence.

After a few days of hesitation, I approached my boss. "Sir, I've been observing the canteen. The amount of food waste is quite high. May I try something to address it?"

He looked at me with interest—and a bit of scepticism.

"What do you have in mind?" "I want to run a cartoon campaign," I said. He paused. "Cartoons?"

"Yes. Something people will stop and look at. Smile at. But also think about—without feeling judged." To my pleasant surprise, he agreed. And that's where things began to change. It was a surprisingly simple intervention—almost playful.

Every morning, I came in early and drew a cartoon on the cafeteria whiteboard—linking the previous day's food waste with humour, current events, and relatable situations.

The numbers were already displayed. But numbers don't move people. Emotion does. Soon, the board became a daily stop. Employees gathered, read, laughed, and discussed. And slowly, behaviour began to shift. Slowly, people began noticing their own habits without feeling judged. Behavioural change becomes easier when people feel included rather than corrected.

People took smaller portions. Waste reduced. Awareness increased. By the end of the year, daily food waste had dropped from **1,500 kilos to under 10 kilos**. No penalties. No enforcement. Just awareness.

We didn't force change. We made people see it.

CHAPTER 36

The Paper Punch Story

"Efficiency is doing better what is already being done."

Peter Drucker

Some lessons don't come from training programs or senior leaders. They arrive quietly—and stay with you for life.

This was one of them.

I had just moved into my first hotel job, transitioning from a manufacturing setup into a five-star front office environment. Everything felt different. The pace, the expectations, the attention to detail—nothing was casual anymore.

Like every new recruit, I was given a basic task to start with: punch and file a stack of reservation forms.

Simple enough, I thought.

I picked up the paper punch and got to work—confident, efficient, and completely unaware that I was doing it all wrong. I punched the papers wherever it felt convenient. Some near the top, some slightly off-centre, some uneven altogether. The result? Chaos.

Papers sticking out at odd angles. Files looking bulky and unprofessional. Nothing aligned. It looked less like organised documentation and more like a badly assembled scrapbook.

When my manager came back and glanced at the files, his reaction said everything. He didn't shout. He didn't correct me directly.

Which somehow made it worse. I knew I had messed up. I just didn't know how.

Around 11:15 that morning, the canteen assistant walked in with my tea, as he did every day- delivering tea across departments.

He placed the cups down, glanced at my desk, and paused.

"Is this how you punch and file papers?" he asked. I didn't take it well.

Here I was, a management trainee, being questioned by someone I subconsciously placed much lower in the hierarchy.

I brushed him off.

But he didn't walk away.

Instead, he picked up the paper punch and pointed at something I had completely missed.

"Do you see this triangle here?" he asked.

I hadn't.

"That's your guide," he said calmly.
"Align the paper to this—and your holes will always be perfect."

He demonstrated it once.

That was all it took.

I tried it immediately after he left.

The difference was instant.

The holes aligned perfectly.
The papers sat neatly.
The file looked professional.

Same tool.
Different understanding.

Later, when my manager returned, he noticed the improvement.

“Good,” he said. “You’ve picked it up.”

I nodded—but I knew where the learning had come from.

That day stayed with me. Because the lesson wasn’t about a paper punch. It was about perspective. Sometimes operational excellence is nothing more than refusing to tolerate avoidable inconvenience.

Wisdom doesn’t follow hierarchy.
It shows up wherever you’re willing to learn.

CHAPTER 37

The Diesel Generator Story Overheard

"Whether you think you can, or you think you can't -you're right."

Henry Ford

Some of the most powerful lessons aren't taught in classrooms or training sessions. They are overheard—unexpected, unfiltered, and deeply revealing. This was one of those moments.

In 2011, I was in Trichy for a training assignment. Like most business trips back then, I checked into a modest hotel—nothing unusual. But the timing was.

Power cuts were a part of everyday life then. Long outages, sometimes scheduled, sometimes not. Businesses had adapted, but not without effort.

One evening, during a power cut, the hotel went unusually quiet. That's when I heard a conversation. An older man called out to a younger employee.

"Come here," he said. "I'll show you how to start the generator."

It sounded like a simple, helpful gesture. The response wasn't.

"I don't want to learn," the younger man said bluntly. There was no hesitation. No curiosity.

The older man tried again. "Just listen," he said patiently.
"You never know when you might need it."

The younger man turned and asked a question that changed the entire tone of the exchange. "If I learn this, will I get paid more?"

That was his filter. If the answer was no, the learning had no value.

The older man paused. Then said quietly, "If you look at everything only from a money point of view, you won't go very far."

The younger man didn't agree. "This job is enough for this salary," he said. "Don't expect more from me." And just like that, the conversation ended. But the lesson didn't. They didn't know anyone was paying attention to the conversation. It was one of those accidental moments that tells you more about a workplace than formal reviews ever can.

Standing there in the dark, I realised I had just witnessed two completely different approaches to growth. The generator wasn't really the story anymore. The mindset around it was.

The older man saw learning as an investment—something that compounds over time, often without immediate reward.

The younger man saw it as a transaction—effort in exchange for instant return.

One mindset builds capability. The other negotiates comfort.

Over the years, I've seen this play out repeatedly. The difference in careers rarely comes from intelligence alone. It comes from attitude towards learning.

Some people prepare before opportunity arrives. Others wait to be rewarded before they begin. The outcomes are rarely the same.

Organizations reveal their real culture in everyday conversations, not in proud proclamations.

Careers don't grow when you get paid more.
They grow when you learn more—before you're paid for it.

CHAPTER 38

The Elderly German Couple Story

"Kindness is a language the deaf can hear and the blind can see."

Mark Twain

In hospitality, we often speak about going "above and beyond." But those words only mean something when someone chooses to act on them. This is one such story.

Our hotel regularly hosted a group of elderly German travellers who visited Chennai as part of a cultural itinerary. They weren't typical tourists. They valued simplicity, authenticity, and human connection.

They came back year after year. During one visit, things took an unexpected turn. An elderly lady from the group fell ill. Not serious—but enough to disrupt the travel plan. The next day, her husband also fell unwell. The group had a decision to make.

Wait and disrupt everyone's schedule—or move ahead. The couple chose to stay back.

Ten days. In a foreign country. Unwell. Alone.

It could have been a lonely and stressful experience. That's when Joel stepped in. Joel was our youngest bellboy. He had no obligation to get involved beyond basic service.

But he noticed something others didn't—their vulnerability.

"Sir, can I help them?" he asked. I agreed—with one condition.

His regular duties should not suffer. He didn't just manage. He committed. Over the next ten days, Joel became everything the couple needed.

He accompanied them to the hospital. Helped them with medicines. Coordinated food. Stayed available—almost around the clock. Not because he was instructed to. Because he cared.

Some colleagues questioned him. Why so much effort for just two guests? Joel never answered them. He simply continued.

By the time the couple recovered, they were deeply grateful. But what happened next was something none of us expected.

Six months later, they returned. Not as guests. But with a decision.

They had initiated the legal process to adopt Joel and take him to Germany. A bellboy—now stepping into a completely new life.

New opportunities.
New environment. A different future altogether.

Years later, Joel came back to visit us. He had settled well. Learnt the language. Built a life. But he remembered where it all started.

Not with opportunity. But with intent.

He didn't just serve guests. He showed up when it mattered.

And that changed everything.

CHAPTER 39

The Malayalam Movie Stars Story

"Hospitality is making your guests feel at home even when you wish they were."

Unknown

In business, there are moments when decisions go beyond process. They become a test of judgment. This was one of those moments.

We were running a small hotel in Chennai, trying to establish ourselves in a competitive market. Every opportunity mattered.

One evening, I received a call from a neighbouring hotel.

"We're full tonight," they said. "We have a few guests from the Malayalam film industry. Can you accommodate them?"

It was exactly the kind of opportunity we were looking for. I agreed immediately. The arrangement was simple—the agent would handle payments. We would provide the stay.

Four guests checked in. For the first few days, everything seemed normal. Then things began to change. The agent became unreachable. Calls weren't returned. Promises weren't kept.

By Day 6, the bill had touched ₹70,000. And there was still no sign of payment. To put that in perspective, my monthly salary at the time was ₹5,000. This wasn't a small gap. This was a serious risk.

I had to address it. When I spoke to the guests, the reality became clear. They weren't established stars. They were upcoming artists—talented but financially stretched. They hadn't been paid.

"We'll settle this once we return home," they said. "We just need a dignified exit." I had two choices.

Hold them back and protect the hotel. Or trust them—and take the risk. There was no guarantee.

But something in their honesty, their discomfort, and the way they handled the situation made the decision clear. I chose to trust them.

They left. The next few days were tense. Had I made the right call? Or an expensive mistake? On the eighth day, the first payment arrived. Then another. And another. Until the full amount was cleared.

Along with a message: "Thank you for trusting us when we needed dignity." That experience stayed with me.

Because it reinforced something simple, but powerful.

Trust carries risk.
But when placed well—it builds something far stronger than control.

CHAPTER 40

The Costly Wait Story

"Great selling is not about pushing products. It is about reading situations."

Unknown

Some of the best lessons in selling come when you're not planning to learn anything. This was one of those moments.

I had reached a mall an hour early for a meeting. With time to kill, I walked into a clothing store—just to pass time. I had no intention of buying anything. And I was prepared. If approached, I would say, "I'm just looking." Simple. Standard. Safe.

But the salesperson didn't ask me that question. Instead, he said, "Sir, are you looking for a casual shirt or a formal one?" It was a subtle shift. He didn't ask if I wanted to buy it. He assumed I already had. Without realising it, I responded. "Formal." That was it. The conversation had moved forward—without resistance. What followed was seamless. He showed options. Observed my reactions. Adjusted quickly.

When I didn't respond to standard designs, he didn't push harder. He pivoted. "Sir, we have something interesting," he said. "A shirt you can reverse—two styles in one." He demonstrated it. One side. Then flipped inside out. A completely different look. Simple idea. Smart presentation. And suddenly, I was interested.

What started as time-pass became engagement. Engagement became decision. I bought the shirt. ₹3,000. I walked out slightly amused—and deeply impressed.

Because what he did wasn't aggressive selling. It was structured thinking. He reframed the conversation. He removed my exit. He guided me without pushing.

He didn't sell me a shirt.
He made it easy for me to say yes.

CHAPTER 41

The Lady at a Wayside Restaurant

"Success is the sum of small efforts repeated day in and day out."

Robert Collier

Great service doesn't need infrastructure. It needs intent.

We were driving from Chennai to Trivandrum when hunger forced us to stop at a small roadside restaurant. You probably wouldn't pick that place. It was a place you ended up at.

The setup was basic. The surroundings modest. Expectations were low. But within minutes, everything changed. The lady running the place welcomed us warmly.

She guided us to wash our hands, arranged seating, and ensured we were comfortable before we even looked at the menu. It wasn't formal. It was natural.

My daughter, like most kids, was picky about food. She watched quietly. Then said, "Don't worry. I know what children like."

She didn't ask what we wanted. She understood what we needed. There was nothing theatrical about her service. Just quiet attentiveness.

She walked into the kitchen and spoke to the cook. What came out wasn't just food—it was thoughtful preparation. Fresh, customised, and exactly right. The quality surprised us. The care stayed with us. When

I tried to tip her, she refused. “I’m just doing my job,” she said. And she meant it.

No performance.
No expectation.

Just pride in doing things right. That experience stayed with me. Because it reminded me of something we often overlook.

Service excellence isn’t about where you work. It’s about how you work. Professionalism does not always come from training programs. Sometimes it comes from pride in one’s work.

You don’t need luxury to create impact.

You need intent.

CHAPTER 42

The Trivandrum Auto on Meter Story

"Integrity is doing the right thing, even when no one is watching."

C.S. Lewis

Some stories are so common in India that they almost become predictable. Different cities. Same script.

This was one of them—until it wasn't.

I had just arrived at Trivandrum railway station at around 6:45 a.m. As I stepped out, I was greeted by a familiar scene—auto drivers surrounding passengers, calling out destinations, negotiating aggressively, and quoting fares that had very little to do with the actual meter.

It's a ritual most Indian travellers know well. You negotiate. They justify. You settle somewhere in between—usually unsure if you've been overcharged. I approached one driver and asked for the fare. He quoted nearly three times the expected amount.

"That's too high," I said. "Meter rate would be much lower." "Sir, I won't get a return passenger," he replied confidently. "I have to charge for both ways." The logic sounded reasonable—until you examined it. "Even then, it should be double, not triple," I said.

He didn't miss a beat. "Sir, it's early morning."

That, apparently, justified everything. I moved on—disappointed but not surprised. Just then, another auto approached from the other side. The driver signalled me. "Where do you want to go, sir?" I told him. Like most passengers, I mentally prepared myself for the usual fare negotiation at the end. Without a word, he turned on the meter.

No negotiation.
No explanation.
No drama.

Just... honesty.

The contrast was striking.

As we drove through the city, something felt different. For once, I wasn't calculating fares in my head. I wasn't preparing for an argument at the end of the ride.

There was trust.

When we reached, the meter read ₹64. I handed him ₹100.

Without hesitation, he reached into his pocket to return the exact change.

That sealed it. "Keep the change," I said.

He accepted it—not greedily, not expectantly—but with quiet gratitude. That short ride stayed with me.

Because in an environment where overcharging had become normal, honesty stood out—not just as ethics, but as strategy.

He didn't argue.
He didn't negotiate.
He didn't try to maximise one transaction.

He made the experience effortless.

And that's what made it memorable. People remember fairness because it creates relief.

In a world used to being overcharged, fairness feels like premium service.

CHAPTER 43

The Bangalore Street Banana Vendor Story

"Common sense is genius dressed in work clothes."

Ralph Waldo Emerson

Some of the most powerful lessons in business don't come from boardrooms. They come from the street.

In Bangalore, near the railway station, there was an 84-year-old banana vendor I would often stop by to see. His cart was small, his setup simple—but his presence was constant. Over time, what began as casual purchases turned into conversations. And those conversations revealed something deeper. He had the alertness of someone constantly reading people.

One evening, around 10 PM, I noticed him handing bananas to a passerby—a beggar.

No hesitation.
No calculation.

Just quiet generosity.

Later, as closing time approached, he continued giving away bananas. Not spoiled fruit. Not leftovers. Perfectly good bananas. Curious, I asked him why. His answer was simple.

"If I can't sell them, why throw them? Someone else can use them."

But what struck me more was not his generosity—it was his mindset. At 84, he didn't need to work. His children were well-settled. He could have comfortably stayed at home.

But he chose not to.

"I want to take care of myself," he said.
"As long as I can."

There was dignity in that decision. There was also sharp business insight.

"I never sit," he told me.

"If I sit, customers won't come."

He understood something many retailers miss—perception matters. To him, standing wasn't just physical effort. It was a signal of readiness. Watching him felt like watching a masterclass in practical customer psychology.

He also spoke multiple languages—picked up over time, out of necessity. Not from formal education. From interaction.

From survival. From intent. His small cart wasn't just a business.

It was independence.
It was identity.
It was purpose.

In eight square feet of space, he had built something most people spend a lifetime searching for—control over his work, dignity in his effort, and meaning in his contribution.

Business wisdom is not restricted to legacy businesses or business schools.

Entrepreneurship isn't about scale.
It's about ownership—of effort, of purpose, of self.

CHAPTER 44

The Magic Housekeeper at GRT

"Do ordinary things extraordinarily well."

Gregg Harris

Great service rarely announces itself. It shows up quietly—in small, consistent moments.

I was walking through the lobby of GRT Hotel on my way to a session when a housekeeper greeted me.

"Namaste."

Simple. Warm. Genuine. Unforced. It didn't feel like a routine greeting. It felt like I was being welcomed. That stayed with me. She carried herself with the calm confidence of someone who knew her work mattered.

As the day progressed, I began noticing something similar across the hotel. The service wasn't exceptional in bursts—it was consistently good. Guests may not have noticed every detail consciously, but they definitely felt the difference.

That made me curious. During a break, I asked the leadership team:

"How do you maintain this level of consistency—especially in departments like housekeeping?"

The answer was simple. A system called the **Bravo Card**.

Employees earned recognition points whenever they went beyond expectations—whether for guests or colleagues.

These points were converted into valuable rewards.

But the real strength wasn't the idea.

It was the consistency.

Everyone was included.
Everyone was observed.
Everyone was recognised.

No hierarchy in appreciation. Only in effort.

That changes behaviour.

When people know their actions matter, they begin to act differently. Not because they are told to—but because they want to.

The greeting I experienced was no longer random.

It was the outcome of a system. Over time, it shaped the culture of the hotel. Employees noticed opportunities to help instead of waiting for instructions. Guests experienced warmth without knowing why. The Bravo Card not only rewarded performance, it reinforced pride, ownership and the understanding that the smallest gesture could create an impact.

Consistency isn't accidental. It is designed.

CHAPTER 45

The Gang at Ooty

"Consistency is not built through intention. It is built through attention."

Unknown

We all have places we go back to.
Not because they are exceptional—but because they are reliable.

This restaurant in Ooty was one of those places for me.

Until one visit changed that.

The moment I walked in, something felt off.

Eight staff members were sitting together, watching something on their phones, laughing loudly.

No one acknowledged me.

I had to walk up and ask,
"Are you open?"

"It is," someone said—without even looking up.

That set the tone.

I placed my order. No engagement. No suggestions.

Just indifference.

As I waited, I observed.

Staff were grouped by language, chatting about movies, personal issues, anything but work.

No ownership.
No coordination.
No leadership presence.

When it was time to pay, the counter was empty.

I had to interrupt them again.

What struck me wasn't just poor service. It was how quickly things had deteriorated.

This wasn't one bad employee. This was a system collapse.

Standards had slipped.
Accountability had disappeared.
And behaviour had followed.

Because once indifference becomes normal, it becomes culture. I didn't return. Not because of one bad experience.

But because the intent was gone.

Reputation is built slowly.
But it collapses quietly—and quickly.

CHAPTER 46

The Security Guard Lesson at the Warehouse

"If you think training is expensive, try ignorance."

Derek Bok

Sometimes, the biggest operational failures come from the simplest misunderstandings.

We had shifted our warehouse to the outskirts of the city—more space, lower cost, better logistics.

On paper, it was a good decision.

One day, we urgently needed supplies. We called the warehouse.

No response.

After repeated attempts, we decided to go there ourselves.

When we arrived, the gate was locked.

Inside, the security guard was asleep—stretched across two chairs, cap over his face.

We tried everything to wake him.

Nothing worked. Finally, someone climbed the wall and woke him up. He opened the gate casually.

No apology.
No urgency.

I asked him,
"How are you sleeping on duty?"

His answer was revealing.

"Sir, this is my first job," he said.
"The previous guard trained me."

He then explained how to arrange chairs, lie down comfortably, and use the cap to block light.

He had been trained.

Just not on the job.

No one had explained his responsibility.
No one had explained the impact of his role.

So, he followed what he was shown.

Perfectly.

That day made something very clear.

Training without context is dangerous.

People don't just need instructions.
They need understanding.

Because if they don't understand the purpose,
they will create their own version of the job.

And that version can be completely wrong.

Compliance without clarity is a risk.
Not a strength.

CHAPTER 47

The Watchman Who Wept Story

"Every person you meet is fighting a battle you know nothing about."

Unknown

Some people don't resist change. They resist connection.

We were conducting a training session with a mixed group—sales staff, warehouse employees, and support teams.

Among them was a watchman who stood out immediately.

Not because of participation. Because of resistance. He was the kind of person most people would notice only in passing.

He sat apart. Spoke little. Avoided engagement. His presence created distance.

When we asked about him, we learnt he worked in isolation. Minimal interaction. Minimal connection.

We moved ahead with the session.

One activity involved giving each group chocolates and asking them to end up with "more."

The idea was simple—collaboration.

The outcomes weren't.

Some tried to grab.
Some negotiated.
Some argued.

And one man did nothing.

He sat alone.

Disconnected.

That's when something unexpected happened.

A young woman walked up to him gently.

"Appa," she said. "Can you give me a chocolate?"

Something shifted.

He gave it. Immediately.

And then, he broke down. The emotion caught everyone slightly off guard. Not quietly. Completely.

When we asked why, his answer was heartbreaking.

"In 63 years, I have never given anything to anyone," he said. "I have lived alone. Fought alone."

His resistance wasn't attitude. It was history.

That one word—"Appa"—had done something no training could. In that moment, he stopped being 'the watchman' and became a human being with fears, pride, and vulnerability."

It gave him connection.

Permission.

Belonging.

He left that session a different person.

More open.
More engaged.

Sometimes, people don't need instruction.

They need recognition.

Behind resistance, there is often loneliness.
And sometimes, one moment is enough to change it.

CHAPTER 48

The Toilet Detour Story at Padappai

"Convenience is the silent salesman."

Unknown

Moments of excellence in customer service often show up in the most unexpected places—during ordinary interactions, in how a product is presented, and in how effortlessly an experience is delivered within the environment you operate in. This was one such moment.

I was at a training session at a fuel station when I witnessed what turned out to be a masterclass in customer relationship management and consultative selling.

It was a regular day. Customers were coming in for fuel, snacks, and basic services. The team was following standard service routines, and we were focused on translating training into practice. Then something interesting happened.

A large, premium car drove into the forecourt and parked neatly. The driver stepped out, accompanied by his elderly mother.

This wasn't a quick fuel stop.

As he walked towards the station, I overheard him say to his mother, in a caring tone, "Ma, I drove 40 minutes out of the way to bring you here. Their restrooms are very clean, and their podi idli is excellent—one stone, two mangoes."

That one statement revealed a lot.

Our facility had built a reputation strong enough for customers to make a deliberate detour. Clean restrooms and good food—neither core to fuel retail—had become powerful differentiators.

Once his mother was settled, he moved to the fuel island.

The team began with their standard approach—offering premium fuel.

He agreed.

After the fill, instead of ending the interaction, the attendant made a suggestion:

"Sir, could you please move your vehicle forward? We will do an Under Bonnet Check"

The customer agreed immediately.

There was no hesitation, no suspicion. He trusted the process.

The inspection revealed that the engine oil was in poor condition and needed replacement. The staff explained the situation clearly and showed him the condition of the oil.

He agreed to the change—without questioning the price or seeking a second opinion.

The service continued.

"Sir, while we are working on your car, may we check your wiper blades as well?"

Again, he agreed.

The wipers were worn out and required replacement. That recommendation too was accepted without resistance.

All this while, his wife—who was at the café—began to question him.

"Why are you agreeing to everything?" she asked.
"At least go and check what they're doing."

His response was simple.

"It's Shell. You don't have to check."

That one sentence captured the power of trust.

The final bill was over ₹17,000—for what had started as a restroom stop.

Premium fuel, engine oil, wiper blades, accessories, food, and snacks.

What stood out was not the value of the transaction—but how it happened.

There was no pressure.
No negotiation.
No resistance.

Every recommendation was made professionally, received with trust, and executed smoothly.

The customer never felt sold to.
He felt advised.

This experience reinforced a few important lessons.

Excellence in basic services—like clean restrooms—can create strong entry points for deeper customer relationships.

Structured processes, when executed with intent, build trust—not resistance.

And once trust is established, customers don't question recommendations—they rely on them.

A simple stop became a complete experience.

Because when trust is built, decisions become easy.

People don't buy more because you push.
They buy more because they trust.

CHAPTER 49

The 87% Story - The Premium Product Journey

"People don't buy what you do. They buy why you do it."

Simon Sinek

Achieving business success often means building it on challenging traditional thinking, pushing accepted boundaries, and having the courage to want what seems to be impossible and blatantly disregard the cynics in your industry or on your board. This is the tale of how we turned our meagre 13 percent share into an astounding 87 percent penetration rate of something that the keyword here is learn. Persistency, strategic planning, customer education, and how to believe in the realm of possibility even when others say it is not practical.

Being the first Shell outlet to commence operations in Chennai and only the second in our network, we brought with us the enthusiasm to chart a new territory as well as the pressure of setting standards for forthcoming sites.

Every detail of our operation was observed, quantified and then benchmarked, which saw performance not as just a measure of business success but as an assertion of the viability of our approach altogether.

Firstly, our penetration for premium fuel landed at 13% or so, which I thought was pretty good for such a price-conscious market and with the entrenched patterns of fuel customers. For most customers, gas was a commodity, the cheapest was the best choice, and getting them to pay more for Premium fuel was going to be a tough sale since we'd spent decades building the habit of buying the cheapest fuel.

However, as our network expanded and new outlets began operations, comparisons became inevitable and increasingly uncomfortable. One of the newer outlets was achieving premium penetration rates of over 40%, making our 13% figure look embarrassingly low by comparison.

That pressure increased during network meetings where performance measures were reviewed. What had been acceptable was no longer good enough and we started to get questions about whether we were as focused on selling high-end products as the other guys and whether or not we really knew what our customers wanted.

More nails in the coffin were added when pointed questions were also put forward about why our penetration rates are low. The unspoken critique was clear: if other outlets could hit 40% premium sales, why were we languishing at 13%? Were we not working hard enough? Were we simply not good enough at upselling?

At first, I tried to dismiss these comparisons by demonstrating that percentages were not reasonable metrics to employ. I started quoting Navjot Singh Sidhu's famous metaphor about statistics and bikinis.

That complaint wasn't totally fair- a 40% take up rate at a small destination could in fact be fewer actual litres than our 13% at a high-volume venue. Yet it was only a short-term measure, and the scrutiny was built further with each performance shortfall.

There was a watershed meeting where our low 'market penetration' was discussed at a meeting. The criticism was getting more explicit, and our standing in the network was eroding. Something had to be different, big time different.

We convened an emergency team meeting to talk about what had become more than just a performance problem, but a crisis of credibility. The mood was grim—our jobs and professional reputations were on the line, and baby steps were just not going to cut it.

We brainstormed what eventually became our process for customer education and premium fuel marketing. The approach was all-encompassing, emphasizing direct conversations with customers over inanimate display or promotion.

We agreed that only supervisors and the most experienced staff—what we called the "blue team"—should have customer conversations about premium fuel. This helped us make sure that our most trained and comfortable associates were behind our product and its recommendations.

It was our targeting solution that made all the difference.

Instead of going after the actively fueling, or the next in line, people in line that we knew were busy and focused on the task at hand, we decided to approach the third person in from any line. This was someone who had time to listen, wasn't in a hurry and could absorb information while waiting to be served.

This approach had the added benefit that when we finished pitching the third customer, the others waiting in line behind or in front of them would also overhear our pitch. By the time these people got to the fuel island, they had already listened to our premium fuel benefits 2 times, so they are much MORE likely to upgrade their purchase.

Every service team member was assigned a goal of striking up conversations with 10 people an hour with the intention of having 90-100 conversations with customers during their shift. This systematic method ensured that the activation fulfilled uniformed message repetition and optimal market penetration.

Unfortunately, though we were enthusiastic and well organized, early findings were rather disheartening. We were hovering around 13% penetration (our premium product), and so we started having some doubts about ourselves and what we were doing.

The idea surfaced in a most unlikely way and emphasized the significance of hearing all voices on the team, not just those with titles and years of experience. One of our review meetings: Srinivasan, a CSA, our most silent member who worked as a nightshift only so barely ever really interacted, made a timid comment which turned out to be quite important.

"Sir, masa kadaisi," he murmured in Tamil, which roughly translated to "month end."

His remark was so matter of fact, none of us could sense what it implied at first. When I asked him to explain, he revealed something that had not even occurred to our management team: At our location, the end of every month consistently posted the lowest sales of premium fuel.

After analyzing our monthly sales behaviour, we, too, found Srinivasan was dead right. Customer buying habits were hugely affected by month-end, with people running out of money and becoming super price-sensitive."

This insight revolutionized our approach. Instead of sustaining pressure all month, we focused our efforts early when clients had more to spend and adjusted our expectations later in the month.

Well, with that new motivation and information in hand, we restarted the campaign to get customers engaged. The results were swift and stunning. Our penetration premium leapt overnight from 13% to 40% and was now approaching that of some of the outlets that had previously been achieving higher penetration than us.

But we didn't stop there. That was success that gave us the momentum and confidence that we needed to take it to the next level. Here, within three months of doing it hard, we'd penetrated over 50% and were now heading for 60%.

The change went beyond anything we had dared to hope for. Regardless of initial feasibility, we ultimately achieved outstanding penetration rates. Customers started to ask for premium fuel, and a few even grumbled if they happened to be there the day we ran out of premium fuel (which was a far cry from how selling premium fuel used to go).

We were probably remembered most for the time we dreamt of decanting a whole truck of premium fuel, (24 KL) in a day – but we ended up adding another compartment of 4KL to our dream and ended up decanting 28,000 litres of Premium product in a day. That volume was unheard of in our network and signified a 180-degree market position change for us.

This experience has left us with some of our core lessons on business transformation and goal attainment. Seems impossible Firstly, impossible dreams become possible when you persistently and creatively pursue them. Second, the most valuable ideas often come from the least expected sources, and it takes leaders who listen to everyone on staff, no matter what they say on the business card.

Third, the insights lead to significant increases in strategy effectiveness when armed with a knowledge of customer behaviour patterns—such as month-end budget constraints. Finally, there's a virtuous cycle: as customers observe other customers choosing premium options and observe that the quality remains continually high, there is rapid widespread adoption.

Our 87% premium penetration rate became the stuff of legends within our system, but it showed that with the correct mindset, hard work, and never missing an opportunity to learn from everyone on the team, even the most audacious goals are within reach. The shift happened when customers began understanding the benefit instead of just hearing the price. Customers are often more open to premium choices than employees initially assume.

Breakthroughs don't always come from strategy.
Sometimes, they come from attention.

CHAPTER 50

The Tirupur Waiter

"People will forget what you said, forget what you did,
but never forget how you made them feel."

Maya Angelou

Great service doesn't need training manuals. Sometimes, it just needs intent. In Tirupur, I found a small restaurant I kept returning to.

Not because of the place. Because of one waiter. He stood out immediately.

Energy. Focus. Precision.

He remembered orders. Preferences. Details.

"Less spicy, sir."
"Extra gravy."

He didn't just serve food. He personalised it.

He also upsold—but effortlessly. He moved quickly, but never in a way that made customers feel rushed."

"Mint lime juice will balance this," he would suggest.

Customers agreed. Not because he pushed.

Because he understood. On my second visit, he remembered me.

“Same as yesterday—or something different?” That changed everything.

He wasn’t serving.

He was guiding. There was attentiveness in the way he noticed tables without hovering around them.

On later visits, he wasn’t there. The difference was obvious.

Service dropped. Energy vanished.

He had made the place special.

Not the other way around.

He once mentioned his mentor.

“He never asked for tips,” he said.
“But earned them.”

That’s the difference.

People may visit establishments for food, but they return for how they are treated.

Great service isn’t taught.
It’s practised—every single time.

Afterword

Greed or Growth – The MORE Journey

As we conclude these 50 stories, the line between greed and growth has become graphically evident. The people you've met—from the witty petrol pump attendant who guessed a customer's biscuit choice to Ramesh who made his hearing loss an advantage—selecting growth over greed. They sought "MORE" not to take away from others, but to build value for all concerned.

The common thread of wisdom in these stories is clear: durable "MORE" happens when we serve, create and genuinely care. It was not an act of taking more for the young store assistant assisting a grandfather in completing his family ceremonial outfit, nor Venkateshwari sharing a smile that could light up even your worst day with every customer interaction despite her own troubles, nor the German couple warmly inviting Joel to theirs from recognition of his exceptional service. This, to me, is the essence of a MORE journey—our most satisfying handiwork does not derive from what we are able to extract out of opportunities but rather from what we are able to infuse into them. For as all of these stories show, if we put service first and foremost our lives will become so abundant.

Implementing MORE In Your Life and Business

The concepts that you've learnt from these anecdotes aren't limited to certain industries or functions—they're universal principles waiting to be applied to any circumstance in which human beings engage with a sense of purpose.

Begin with observation. As the Shell employee selling Nutrichoice did, get into the habit of observing what people require prior to their asking. As a leader of a team, customer service provider, or relationship builder, outstanding outcomes start with outstanding awareness.

Seize limitations as drivers. Ramesh's special ability became the starting point for groundbreaking customer service systems. Your limitations, in the right mindset, can be your biggest strengths. Seek out the ingenuity hiding in your challenges.

Make personal connections. The Nafeez Latte and Nirankari Baba Doppio anecdotes remind us that individuals desire to be noticed and appreciated as human beings. In a world of automation, the personal touch becomes ever more valuable and mightier.

Take ownership of outcomes. The Ulundurpet associate who demanded the master prepare fresh snacks demonstrated that excellence requires personal responsibility. Don't wait for permission to solve problems or create better experiences.

Question assumptions. The Thaltej and Maninagar teams discovered hidden opportunities by challenging conventional wisdom about their markets. What "impossible" improvements might be waiting in your environment?

Looking Forward: The Power of Continuous Improvement

The most inspiring part of these stories is that they are beginnings, not conclusions. Each of the individuals who decided to do more sent out a ripple effect that touched thousands more. The watchman who learnt to give, the security guard who found his calling, the innumerable customers who encountered service beyond expectations—all were part of an ever-growing circle of excellence.

This is your invitation to join that circle. Each interaction you have today holds the choice of adequate or exceptional, transaction or transformation, good enough or MORE.

The magic of ongoing improvement is not in flawless implementation but in persistent resolve. Begin where you find yourself, with what you have available to you, and vow to bring just a little more focus, care, and imagination to your next chance to serve others.

Remember: the power of MORE isn't something you do more of—it's something you become more of. When you choose this path, you don't just get better results; you become part of the solution to making the world a little better, one interaction at a time.

MORE's journey starts with one decision: to offer more of yourself to what you're doing at this exact moment. All that remarkableness that comes next begins with that one simple, yet mighty, decision.

MORE POWER TO YOU!!

About the Author

Manoj Kumar is a hospitality professional, trainer, and entrepreneur who has spent decades working at the intersection of service, sales, and people development across hotels, restaurants, and retail environments.

His journey began on the frontlines—observing customers, handling operations, solving everyday service challenges, and working closely with teams that form the backbone of the industry. Over the years, he moved into leadership and training roles, working with organisations across hospitality, fuel retail, and service sectors, helping them build stronger teams, improve customer experience, and drive sustainable business outcomes.

What sets Manoj apart is his deep engagement with entry-level and frontline employees—the waiters, pump attendants, housekeeping staff, sales associates, and service crew who directly influence customer experience but are often the least trained and least supported.

Through years of training, coaching, and field immersion, he has seen firsthand how small, consistent inputs—when delivered well—can transform not just performance, but confidence, dignity, and long-term career growth.

Why This Book

This book was built on highways, in cafés, at petrol pumps, inside hotel lobbies, retail stores, and training rooms—through real conversations, real people, and real situations. Across his journey, Manoj noticed a pattern.

Leaders, managers, and supervisors often receive structured training, mentoring, and exposure throughout their careers. They are taught frameworks, strategies, and decision-making tools.

But the people at the entry level—the ones who interact with customers every day—rarely receive the same level of attention.

They are expected to perform without being fully prepared. They are expected to stay motivated without being consistently guided.

They are expected to grow without being shown how. The Gap That Needed Attention

In industries like hospitality and retail, with low entry barriers, the first few months of a job are critical.

This is where:

- Confidence is either built—or broken
- Habits are formed
- Attitudes towards work are shaped

For many entry-level employees, this phase is overwhelming.

They deal with:

- Language barriers
- Fear of making mistakes
- Lack of clarity in expectations
- Minimal structured guidance
- High-pressure environments

Self-doubt sets in quickly. And when that happens, exits follow.

High attrition is not just a hiring problem—it is a training and support problem.

The Purpose Behind This Work

This book is Manoj's attempt to bridge that gap.

Not through theory.

But through stories.

Stories that show:

- What great service looks like in real life
- How small actions create large impact
- How ordinary people deliver extraordinary outcomes
- How "a little more" changes everything

These are not idealized examples. They are lived experiences.

They come from people who did not have perfect English, elite education, or corporate exposure—but had the willingness to observe, care, and act.

Beyond the Book: Building for Scale

While stories inspire, Manoj recognised that inspiration alone is not enough. Sustained change requires consistent reinforcement.

To address this, he is building a digital skilling platform-Skilld'wise (app-based) designed specifically for:

- Blue-collar workforce
- Entry-level staff in hospitality and retail
- Frontline service teams

The goal is simple:

To deliver continuous, practical, easy-to-consume training that fits into their daily work lives.

What Makes This Approach Different

Unlike traditional training programs that are:

- One-time
- Classroom-heavy
- Difficult to sustain

This approach focuses on:

- Microlearning
- Real-life scenarios
- Simple frameworks
- Repeatable behaviours

It recognizes that:

Skill is not built in a session. It is built through repetition, relevance, and reinforcement.

A Larger Vision. At its core, this work is about respect.

Respect for the people who:

- Stand on their feet all day
- Serve without recognition
- Learn through doing, not instruction
- Carry the brand experience on their shoulders

When they are trained well:

- Customer experience improves
- Business performance improves
- Lives improve

And most importantly,
they begin to see themselves differently.

A Simple Belief

If entry-level employees receive the same level of structured guidance, coaching, and encouragement that leaders receive, they will not just stay longer.

They will grow faster. Perform better. And take pride in what they do.

Final Thought

This book is a collection of stories. But behind every story is a simple idea:

When people are shown how to give a little more, they don't just do better work - they build better lives.

This is not just a book about service. It is about people. And what becomes possible when they are given the right start.

DO MORE | CREATE MAGIC | MORE POWER TO YOU

www.ingramcontent.com/pod-product-compliance
Lightning Source LLC
LaVergne TN
LVHW022216200926
848481LV00006B/1995